Catholic Christianity

REVISION GUIDE

VICTOR W. WATTON

Hodder Murray
A MEMBER OF THE HODDER HEADLINE GROUP

The publishers would like to thank the following individuals, institutions and companies for permission to reproduce copyright illustrations in this book: © Bettmann/Corbis, page 53; © Ralf Finn Hestoft/Corbis, page 59; © Jim Holmes/CAFOD, page 70.

Every effort has been made to trace and acknowledge ownership of copyright. The publishers will be glad to make suitable arrangements with any copyright holders whom it has not been possible to contact.

Note about the Internet links in the book. The user should be aware that URLs or web addresses change regularly. Every effort has been made to ensure the accuracy of the URLs provided in this book on going to press. It is inevitable, however, that some will change. It is sometimes possible to find a relocated web page by just typing in the address of the home page for a website in the URL window of your browser.

Orders: please contact Bookpoint Ltd, 130 Milton Park, Abingdon, Oxon OX14 4SB. Telephone: (44) 01235 827720. Fax: (44) 01235 400454. Lines are open from 9.00–6.00, Monday to Saturday, with a 24 hour message answering service. You can also order through our website www.hodderheadline.co.uk.

A catalogue record for this title is available from the British Library

ISBN 0 340 812 63 X

First Published 2003
Impression number   10 9 8 7 6 5 4
Year   2009 2008 2007 2006 2005

Copyright © 2003 Victor W. Watton.

All rights reserved. No part of this publication may be reproduced or transmitted in any form or by any means, electronic or mechanical, including photocopy, recording, or any information storage and retrieval system, without permission in writing from the publisher or under licence from the Copyright Licensing Agency Limited. Further details of such licences (for reprographic reproduction) may be obtained from the Copyright Licensing Agency Limited, of 90 Tottenham Court Road, London W1T 4LP.

Hodder Headline's policy is to use papers that are natural, renewable and recyclable products and made from wood grown in sustainable forests. The logging and manufacturing processes are expected to conform to the environmental regulations of the country of origin.

Cover photo from Photodisc.
Typeset by Dorchester Typesetting Group Limited
Printed in Great Britain for Hodder Murray, an imprint of Hodder Education, a member of the Hodder Headline Group, 338 Euston Road, London NW1 3BH by Hobbs The Printers, Totton, Hants.

CONTENTS

How to use this guide for AQA Specification A	2
How to use this guide for Edexcel	3
Exam questions and techniques	4
Chapter 1 Believing in God	7
Chapter 2 Matters of Life and Death	11
Chapter 3 Marriage and Family Life	17
Chapter 4 Social Harmony	23
Chapter 5 Religion and the Media	30
Chapter 6 Religion: Wealth and Poverty	35
Good answers to exam questions for chapters 1–6	39
Chapter 7 Beliefs and Values	46
Chapter 8 Community and Tradition	52
Chapter 9 Worship and Celebration	59
Chapter 10 Living the Christian Life	68
Chapter 11 A Place of Catholic Worship	72
Chapter 12 Christian Vocation	76
Good answers to exam questions for chapters 7–12	81

HOW TO USE THIS GUIDE FOR AQA SPECIFICATION A

The aim of this guide is to help you revise and improve your exam skills so that you attain your highest possible performance in GCSE Religious Studies.

If you are studying Option 1B – Christian Belief and Practice with reference to the Roman Catholic Tradition, you will need to learn:
Chapter 7 (omitting Sin and Salvation, Christian values)
Chapter 8 (omitting Celibacy of the Clergy, Ordination of Women)
Chapter 9
Chapter 11

You will also need to learn about private worship and the Bible, which are not covered in this book.

If you are studying Option 2B – Effects of the Roman Catholic Tradition upon Aspects of Christain Lifestyle and Behaviour, you will need to learn:
Chapter 3
Chapter 4 (omitting Multi-faith Britain)
Chapter 7 (Sin and Salvation and Christian Values only)
Chapter 12 (omitting Purpose and Practice of One Religious Community)

You will also need to learn about crime and punishment and war and peace, which are not covered in this book.

Each chapter is divided into subsections which you should use in the following way:

1. Learn the key words for the subsection.
2. Learn the key facts for the subsection.
3. Learn the main facts for the subsection.
4. Do the practice questions at the end of the chapter and check your answer with the full mark answer to see how you well have done.

If your answers show that you are having problems:

1. Check whether your problem is that you cannot remember the facts. If it is, re-learn the facts.
2. Check whether your problem is that you have not answered the question properly. If it is, re-read the 'Exam questions and techniques' section.

HOW TO USE THIS GUIDE FOR EDEXCEL

The aim of this guide is to help you revise and improve your exam skills so that you attain your highest possible performance in GCSE Religious Studies.

You should read the 'Exam questions and techniques' section first so that you know what types of questions are asked by Edexcel and what sort of answers are expected. You should then work through chapters 1–4 which cover all the compulsory sections of the Edexcel exam paper for Unit C. If you are not doing coursework, you should then work through either chapter 5 or chapter 6 (whichever option you have been taught). You should then work through chapters 7–10, which cover all the compulsory sections of the Edexcel exam paper for Unit J. If you are not doing coursework, you should then work through either chapter 11 or chapter 12 (whichever option you have been taught).

Each of these chapters is a section of the Edexcel specification (syllabus) on which you will **have** to answer a question in the exam. Each of these chapters is divided into subsections, which you should use in the following way:

1. Learn the key words for the subsection.
2. Learn the key facts for the subsection.
3. Learn the main facts for the subsection.
4. Do the practice questions at the end of the chapter and check your answer with the full mark answer in Good answers to exam questions for chapters 1–6 and Good answers to exam questions for chapters 7–12 to see how well you have done.

If your answers show that you are having problems:

1. Check whether your problem is that you cannot remember the facts. If it is, re-learn the appropriate chapter.
2. Check whether your problem is that you have not answered the question properly. If it is, re-read the 'Exam questions and techniques' section.

EXAM QUESTIONS AND TECHNIQUES

The examination paper is divided into five sections if you are not doing coursework, and four sections if you are doing coursework.

In each section you will have a choice of two questions:

Section 1: question 1 or 2

Section 2: question 3 or 4

Section 3: question 5 or 6

Section 4: question 7 or 8

Section 5: question 9 or 10

Techniques for choosing questions

Tick the parts of the question you think you can get a good mark on, giving more ticks for parts you feel more confident about, 1 tick for (a), 3 ticks for (b), 4 ticks for (c), and 2 ticks for (d).

Add up the ticks and choose the question which has the most ticks.

Remember! You have **to choose a complete question**. This means that you must answer all parts (a), (b), (c) and (d) in your chosen question.

Types of questions in sections 1–4

All the questions have part (a) for 2 marks, part (b) for 6 marks, part (c) for 8 marks and part (d) for 4 marks.

Part (a) questions

These are short-answer knowledge questions. You do not need to write full sentences for your answers. You will need to know the meanings of the key words for these questions.

Part (b) questions

These are knowledge questions, which require a one or two paragraph answer.

They will usually begin with **outline** or **describe**:

- **Outline** means you write one or two sentences about a number of issues. For example, 'Outline the types of religious experience' means to write a sentence on each of the following: numinous, miracles and conversion.

- **Describe** means to write in depth about one particular issue. For example, 'Describe one religious experience' means write one or two paragraphs on one particular religious experience someone has had.

- If you are asked to outline different attitudes, it means you must write about at least two attitudes.

Part (a) = not many words needed, one or two sentences

Part (b) = more words needed, one or two paragraphs.

Part (c) questions

These are all understanding questions and usually begin with the word **explain**.

You must go through the question and highlight the key words, which tell you how to write your answer:

- **Why** means you must use the word 'because' and give reasons. For example, 'Explain why some Christians are against divorce' means you must answer in a way such as 'Some Christians are against divorce because they believe that the marriage vows are between the couple and God as well as each other ...' (then go on and give any more reasons you can think of).

- **How** means you must connect two ideas. For example, 'Explain how Catholic teachings could help to promote racial harmony' means you must write out one teaching and explain how it could lead followers of the religion to help racial harmony, then write out another teaching and how it too could lead followers to help racial harmony, and continue in this way.

- **Explain the relationship** needs the same type of answer as 'Explain how'.

When you see the word 'why' start singing the Wizard of Oz song so that you remember BECAUSE, BECAUSE, BECAUSE.

Part (d) questions

These are evaluation questions. They begin with a statement in quotation marks and then ask:

'Do you agree? Give reasons for your opinion, showing that you have considered another point of view'.

Even though the question asks, 'Do you agree?', it is not enough just to give your opinion. You must:

- look at a view which is different from your opinion and say, with reasons, why people have this view;
- state why you agree or disagree with this view using evidence from your knowledge of Religious Studies;
- come to a conclusion restating whether you agree with the question or not with a brief reason.

It is very important that you use religious evidence from the course and that you show you have thought about the statement before coming to a conclusion.

You could use one of the following: quotations from the holy book of one of the religions you have studied; statements from religious leaders; examples from worship or ceremonies; statistics. It is vital that you back up your opinion with religious evidence, and that your answer shows that you have done some 'moral or religious reasoning'.

Example of a good evaluation answer

'Having a religious wedding ceremony makes no difference to how the marriage works out.' Do you agree? Give reasons for your opinion, showing that you have considered another point of view. In your answer, you should refer to Catholic Christianity.

(a) The view you disagree with, and your reasons Many people think that having a religious wedding ceremony makes no difference to how the marriage works out. Such people claim that the figures show marriages that began with a religious ceremony are just as likely to end in divorce as registry office weddings.

(b) Your view, with reasons However, it seems to me that this view ignores a lot of the evidence and so I disagree with the statement in the question. In a Catholic wedding ceremony, the bride and groom have to make promises to each other in the sight of God. They have to promise to love and cherish each other, in sickness and in health, until death parts them. Because they have made these promises to God as well as to each other, they have an extra reason for keeping them. Also a Catholic wedding ceremony involves a homily from the priest, Bible readings about the nature of marriage and how to make it work, and prayers asking for God's help to make the marriage work.

(c) Conclusion So, it seems to me, that religious wedding ceremonies do help to make a marriage work. At the end of the day, a long religious ceremony with promises made to God in front of all your family and friends is bound to have an effect on your marriage.

Types of questions in section 5

If you are not doing coursework, you will have to answer one question from section 5. The maximum number of marks is 23, i.e. 3 marks more than the other questions.

You should spend at least 30 minutes on this question and it is a good idea to do it first so that you do not run out of time on this question.

Part (a) is a knowledge question, the same as the other part (b) questions.

Part (b) is an understanding question, the same as the other part (c) questions, but you should write a longer answer.

Part (c) is an evaluation question, the same as the other part (d) questions, but marks are out of 8 rather than 4 and should have a longer answer.

The extra 3 marks are for your Quality of Written Communication, so make sure you:

- write in sentences;
- use paragraphs;
- do not use slang or bullet points;
- take care with your spelling.

CHAPTER 1
BELIEVING IN GOD

1. You will need to know about Catholic upbringing and belief in God.

MAIN FACTS

If someone is brought up by religious Catholic parents, then they will believe in God from the beginning of their life.

They will be baptised and taken to worship God with their parents. They will be taught to pray to God every day; they will be expected to thank God and remember God's good gifts at various religious festivals, especially at Christmas and Easter. They will go to first communion classes and Children's Liturgies and learn about God. They are likely to go to a Catholic school where everyone believes in God and so they are expected to believe in God.

With an upbringing like this, it is natural to believe in God, and such people might never even consider that God might not exist.

KEY FACTS: Having a religious upbringing leads to belief in God because children are taught that God exists and spend most of their time with people who believe God exists.

Remember! You can use your own Catholic upbringing to answer the questions.

2. You will need to know about religious experience and belief in God.

MAIN FACTS

Religious experience means the ways in which people come into direct contact with God. There are various types of religious experience:

- It can be just a feeling you get when you are in a holy building or say your prayers, or even look up at the stars, and feel in the presence of something greater than yourself. This is called **the numinous**.
- It can be a more definite feeling of God's presence which makes you much more religious and changes your life (for example, St Paul on the road to Damascus). This is called **a conversion** experience.
- It can be believing that **a miracle** has happened, for example, when someone is cured of an incurable disease after prayers have been said for them, or something connected with religion.
- It can be **having a prayer answered**, for example, someone prays for God to help them out of a problem and the problem disappears.

Any of these experiences are almost certain to lead the person who experiences them to believe in God.

KEY WORDS

Numinous	the feeling of the presence of something greater than you, e.g. in a church or looking up at the stars.
Conversion	when someone's life is changed by giving themselves to God.
Miracle	something which seems to break a law of science and for which God seems the only explanation.
Prayer	an attempt to communicate with God, usually through words.

KEY FACTS: People claim to experience God in miracles, answered prayers, the numinous and conversion. Religious experience makes people feel that God is real.

Believing in God   7

3. You will need to know about the appearance of the world and belief in God.

KEY WORDS

Design — when things are connected and seem to have a purpose, e.g. the eye is designed for seeing.

Causation — the idea that everything has been caused (started off) by something else.

KEY FACTS

- The universe seems to be designed and people think that means God must exist because a design needs a designer.
- The way everything seems to have a cause makes people think that the universe must have a cause, which could only be God.

MAIN FACTS

Some people think the way the world works shows that God must exist.

The universe seems to be designed

- The way the universe works according to laws such as gravity.
- The way humans grow from a tiny blueprint of DNA, etc.
- The way the complex mechanism of the eye allows people to see.
- The way the Big Bang worked with the laws of science to produce a universe of order.
- If something is designed, it must have a designer.
- The only possible designer of the universe is God; therefore, they believe God must exist.

The universe needs a cause

- Science says everything has a cause or an explanation. Therefore the universe itself must have a cause.
- Only God could be the cause of the universe. Therefore, God must exist.

4. You will need to know other reasons for believing in God.

KEY FACTS

- Some people believe in God because they believe there must be a reason for humans being here.
- Some people believe God must exist when so many people believe in him.

MAIN FACTS

Many people cannot believe that people are here by chance. They think that life must have a meaning and purpose. Only God and life after death can give life meaning. So God must exist.

The fact that there are religions that seem to believe a lot of the same things about God, and that some people believe in God, shows that God must exist. All those people and religions cannot be wrong.

Does it make something true if lots of people believe it?
Think of how many people used to believe the earth was flat.

8   Catholic Christianity Revision Guide

5. You will need to know why some people do not believe in God.

MAIN FACTS

- Scientific explanations of the world can lead people to become agnostic (not sure whether God exists) or atheist (believing that God does not exist). Science now explains the world and the universe much better than religion. Also the discoveries of astronomy and astronauts going into space make it difficult to think of anywhere God could be.

- Problems with miracles can lead people to become agnostic or atheist. Why would a good God send miracles for a few people, but allow thousands to starve to death and millions to die in the Holocaust? Also most miracles can now be explained.

- Unanswered prayers can lead people to become agnostics or atheists. God is supposed to care for those who worship him and answer prayers, but if someone prays for God to help a dying child and the child dies, that person may well become agnostic or atheist.

- Evil and suffering in the world lead some people to become agnostics or atheists. People suffer from such things as disease, starvation, earthquakes and wars. If God is good, he must want to get rid of such things. If God is all-powerful (omnipotent), he must be able to get rid of such things. The fact that these things continue to exist leads some people to believe that there is no God.

KEY WORDS

| Agnosticism | not being sure whether God exists. |
| Atheism | believing that God does not exist. |

KEY FACTS

Some people do not believe in God because of such things as evil and suffering, unanswered prayers, lack of evidence, scientific explanations of religion, etc.

6. You will need to know about the problem of evil and suffering.

MAIN FACTS

Christians and other religious believers find the existence of evil and suffering a problem because:

- they believe that God is good (benevolent), but if God is good, he ought not to want evil and suffering in his world;
- they believe that God is able to do anything (omnipotent), but if God is all-powerful, he must be able to get rid of evil and suffering from the world he created;
- this means that either God is not good or God is not all-powerful, or else God does not exist.

KEY WORDS

Moral evil	actions done by humans which cause suffering.
Natural evil	things which cause suffering, but have nothing to do with humans, e.g. earthquakes.
Benevolent	the belief that God is good/kind.
Omnipotent	the belief that God is all-powerful/can do anything.
Omniscient	the belief that God knows everything that has happened and everything that will happen.

KEY FACTS

People who believe in God find evil and suffering a problem because God should not want such things to happen. Yet he also ought to be able to get rid of evil and suffering, but he doesn't.

Believing in God

7. You will need to know how Catholics respond to evil and suffering.

KEY FACTS

Catholics respond to evil and suffering by:
- praying for those who suffer;
- helping those who suffer;
- claiming that it is the fault of humans misusing their free will;
- claiming that it is part of a test to prepare people for heaven.

Problem of evil and suffering = why it is a problem for Catholics. **Response to the problem of evil and suffering** = how Catholics explain/deal with the problem.

MAIN FACTS

- Many Catholics respond to the problem by believing that God knows the answer but people cannot. Jesus showed people that God wants them to fight against evil and suffering, so they follow the example of Jesus and pray for those who suffer and give them practical help wherever possible.

- Some Catholics think that God could not give humans free will without giving them the chance to do evil things (being free is part of being made in God's image). Humans have used their free will to do evil things and this has brought suffering into the world. So evil and suffering is the fault of humans not God.

- Other Catholics believe that this life is a sort of test in which people prepare their souls for heaven. If there was no evil and suffering, then they would not be able to develop as good people, because being good involves helping those who suffer and fighting against evil. If people follow the Christian way, then their souls will become good and God will send them to heaven when they die.

- All Christians believe they must respond to suffering by trying to help those who suffer, either by praying for them or by working for CAFOD, becoming a nurse, etc.

Practice questions

(a) What is a miracle? (2)

(b) Describe a religious experience. (6)

(c) Explain how ONE religion responds to the problem of evil and suffering. (8)

(d) 'No one can be sure that God exists.' Do you agree? Give reasons for your opinion, showing you have considered another point of view. (4)

CHAPTER 2
MATTERS OF LIFE AND DEATH

1. You will need to know about Catholic Christianity and life after death.

MAIN FACTS

All Christians believe that this life is not all there is. But Christians differ in their beliefs about what actually happens after death.

1. Catholic teaching on life after death.

The Catholic Church teaches that when people die, the perfectly pure go to heaven, those with unforgiven sins (mainly Christians) go to purgatory to be purified, and everyone else goes to hell. On the Last Day, God will create a new heaven and earth where those from heaven and purgatory will live for ever. Those in hell will stay there. Catholics believe this because:

- it is the teaching of the Church in the *Catechism*;
- purgatory is a fair way of giving everyone another chance;
- this teaching makes sense of the biblical teachings of resurrection of the body and immortality of the soul.

2. Other Christian beliefs about life after death.

Many Evangelical Protestant Christians believe that when people die they stay in the grave until the end of the world when God will raise the dead and judge everyone. True Christians will go to heaven and everyone else will go to hell (though some believe good members of other religions will get another chance). They believe in resurrection of the body because:

- it is what St Paul teaches in *1 Corinthians* 15;
- it was Jesus' body that rose from the dead;
- it is part of the Christian creeds.

Many other Christians believe in the immortality of the soul – that the soul/mind is immortal and lives on after death. When people die their souls go straight to heaven. They believe this because:

- Jesus said the criminal on the cross would be in paradise straight after death;
- the communion of saints teaches that living and dead Christians can communicate with each other;
- things like near-death experiences when people say their soul has left their body and gone down a tunnel of light to God show the immortality of the soul.

KEY WORDS

Resurrection	the belief that, after death, the body stays in the grave until the end of the world when it is raised.
Immortality	the idea that the soul lives on after the death of the body.
Purgatory	a place where Catholics believe souls go after death to be purified.
Heaven	a place of paradise where God rules.
Hell	a place of horrors where Satan rules.
Paranormal	unexplained things which are thought to have spiritual causes, e.g. ghosts, mediums.

KEY FACTS

All Christians believe in life after death because they believe Jesus rose from the dead, and it is part of the teachings of Jesus and the Church.

- Catholics believe that, at death, the pure go to heaven and other Christians go to purgatory until the Last Day when they will go to heaven.
- Some other Christians believe in resurrection – that when they die they will stay in the grave and be raised on the Last Day.
- Some other Christians believe in immortality of the soul – that when the body dies, the soul lives on in heaven.

Matters of Life and Death

Christian beliefs about life after death may differ, but all Christians believe in life after death and this gives their lives purpose and meaning.

3. Why Christians believe in life after death.

All Christians believe that there is life after death because:

- Jesus rose from the dead;
- the Bible says that there is life after death;
- the Churches teach that there is life after death;
- the creeds say there is life after death;
- there is the possibility of life after death as reports of near-death experiences and the paranormal suggest;
- they believe that life after death gives life meaning and purpose.

2. You will need to know why some people do not believe in life after

KEY FACTS

Some people do not believe in life after death because the only evidence is in holy books that contradict each other. They do not see where life after death could take place.

Brain death = when someone's body is alive on a life-support machine, but their brain has died.

MAIN FACTS

Some people do not believe in life after death because:

- the main evidence for life after death is in holy books that contradict each other. For example, the Qur'an says it will be through resurrection; the Gita says it is through reincarnation; some of the Bible says it will be through immortality of the soul;
- no-one has undoubtedly returned from the dead;
- science shows that when the body dies, the brain dies;
- there is no place where life after death could take place;
- life-support machines show that the brain dies, so what could survive death?

3. You will need to know about Christians and contraception.

MAIN FACTS

1. Catholic attitudes to contraception.

The Catholic Church teaches that all forms of artificial contraception are wrong and should not be used because:

- God gave sex for reproduction so every act of sex should be open to the possibility of new life;
- artificial contraception can encourage sexual immorality;
- if sex is restricted to a married couple with no contraception, the family is strengthened.

Some Catholics disagree with the Church's teaching and use contraceptives because the *Catechism* teaches that Catholics can follow their consciences on moral issues, and the Catholic bishops of the USA have said the moral guilt of using contraception can be reduced because of the pressures of modern life.

2. The attitude of other Christians.

Other Christian Churches teach that contraception is an acceptable way of married couples restricting their family size. They believe this because:

- God created sex for the enjoyment of married couples and to help their marriage; therefore it does not have to be connected to reproduction;
- they believe that contraception improves women's health and raises the standard of living of families.

KEY WORD

Contraception preventing conception from occurring.

The rhythm method is a natural form of contraception approved by the Catholic Church.

KEY FACTS

Contraception is using artificial means to prevent a baby being conceived during sex. The Catholic Church teaches that contraception is wrong because God gave sex to create children. Other Christians believe that contraception is allowed because God created sex for a couple to strengthen their marriage.

Matters of Life and Death

4. You will need to know about abortion and the law.

KEY WORDS

Abortion	the removal of a foetus from the womb before it can survive.
Sanctity of life	the belief that life is holy and belongs to God.

KEY FACTS

Abortion is allowed in Great Britain if two doctors agree that there is a medical reason for it. The number of abortions in the UK is going down.

Abortion on demand means that women have the right to an abortion without any questions about the reasons.

MAIN FACTS

The law in Great Britain says that abortion is only allowed if two doctors agree:

- the mother's life is at risk;
- the mother's physical or mental health is at risk;
- the child is very likely to be born severely handicapped;
- there would be a serious effect on other children in the family.

Abortions should not be carried out after 24 weeks of pregnancy.

Most abortions are now carried out on women less than 12 weeks pregnant and the number of abortions has gone down since 1991.

People who argue about abortion often argue about when life begins. Some say it begins:

- as soon as an egg is fertilised;
- when it receives a soul (about 15 weeks);
- when the foetus can survive outside the womb.

Catholic Christianity Revision Guide

5. You will need to know about Christianity and abortion.

MAIN FACTS

There are two different Christian teachings on abortion:

1. Catholic attitudes to abortion.

Catholics, and many Evangelical Protestants, believe abortion is always wrong because:

- Christianity teaches that all life is sacred;
- God has created life in the mother, and to prevent that life being born is murder and against God's will;
- they believe that life begins at conception, and, as God banned murder in the sixth commandment, all abortions should be banned.

2. The attitudes of other Christians.

Other Protestants (for example, the Church of England) and Orthodox Christians disagree with abortion, but think that in certain circumstances it is necessary to choose the lesser of two evils and so abortion must be allowed because:

- they do not believe that life begins at conception;
- they believe Jesus' command to love your neighbour is the most important command;
- they believe it is the duty of Christians to remove suffering;
- they believe that when faced with a choice between two evils, Christians should choose the lesser evil.

KEY FACTS

Christians have different views about abortion:

- Catholics and some Protestant Christians believe that abortion is always wrong because it is murder and against God's will.
- Some Christians believe that abortion is wrong but must be allowed in some circumstances as the lesser of two evils.

The lesser of two evils = when you are faced with a choice where whatever you choose will be wrong, but one choice will be less wrong, e.g. abortion for a girl who has become pregnant through rape.

6. You will need to know about euthanasia.

MAIN FACTS

- Changes in medical skills and technology mean that euthanasia is now more discussed.
- Life-support machines, new medical technology to keep handicapped babies alive, and better drugs to fight cancer mean that people are being kept alive by medicine – often in agony.
- The law says nothing can be done by doctors that could be thought of as euthanasia. However, recent decisions by the courts have allowed doctors to switch off life-support machines and stop feeding patients who are in a persistent vegetative state.

KEY FACTS

There are various types of euthanasia which are all aimed at giving an easy death to those suffering intolerably. It is more of a problem now because medicine can keep people alive who would have died.

Matters of Life and Death

7. You will need to know about Christianity and euthanasia.

KEY WORDS

Euthanasia	an easy and gentle death.
Assisted suicide	providing a seriously ill person with the means to commit suicide.
Voluntary euthanasia	the situation where someone dying in pain asks a doctor to end his/her life painlessly.
Non-voluntary euthanasia	ending someone's life painlessly when they are not able to ask, but you have good reason for believing they would want you to do so, e.g. switching off a life-support machine.

Quality of life = being able to think, communicate with others, feed yourself, be free from severe pain, etc. Some people think that low or no quality of life is a reason for euthanasia.

KEY FACTS

All Christians are against euthanasia because they believe life is sacred and belongs to God. However, there are some different attitudes among Christians about the switching off of life-support machines.

MAIN FACTS

All Christians oppose the practice of euthanasia because:

- they believe that life is sacred and should be taken only by God;
- the Bible says quite clearly that Christians must not murder (sixth commandment);
- there are many statements in the Bible stating that life and death decisions belong to God alone;
- many Church leaders have said that life is sacred and comes from God; therefore, only God can decide when someone should die;
- Christians believe that doctors are required to save lives not kill, and to allow them to kill people would be giving them double standards to follow.

However, there are some different views:

- Most Christians (including Catholics) accept that doctors should be allowed to give lots of painkilling drugs even if they know it is shortening the patient's life. They also believe that expensive treatments need not be carried out to lengthen the lives of dying patients.
- Some Christians do not agree with switching off life-support machines, but many Christians believe this must be allowed when there are no signs of life.

Practice questions

(a) What is immortality? (2)

(b) Outline Christian attitudes to euthanasia. (6)

(c) Explain why there are different beliefs among Christians about life after death. (8)

(d) 'Religious people should never have an abortion.' Do you agree? Give reasons for your opinion, showing you have considered another point of view. (4)

CHAPTER 3
MARRIAGE AND FAMILY LIFE

1. You will need to know about sex and marriage.

MAIN FACTS

Attitudes to sex and marriage have changed greatly in the last 50 years. Fifty years ago sex before marriage and cohabitation were regarded by society as sins, but now:

- many more couples live together before getting married (in 1971, 7% of couples; in 1989, 48%);
- fewer people are getting married (405,000 people married in the UK in 1971; only 299,000 in 1993);
- many more marriages end in divorce (25,000 divorces in 1961; 151,000 divorces in 1991);
- it is accepted that couples will live together before, or instead of, getting married;
- sex before marriage is an accepted part of life.

KEY WORDS

Cohabitation	living together without being married.
Marriage	a man and woman legally joined so that they are allowed to live together for life and, usually, to have children.
Faithfulness	staying with your marriage partner and having sex only with them.
Premarital sex	sex before marriage.
Promiscuity	having sex with a number of partners without wanting a relationship with them.
Adultery	when you are married, having sex with someone other than your marriage partner.

KEY FACTS

Sex before marriage is accepted by society and many couples now live together rather than marrying. Fewer people marry and more marriages end in divorce.

Marriage and Family Life 17

2. You will need to know about Christianity and sex and marriage.

> Remember questions on sex outside marriage mean you have to talk about sex before marriage and adultery.

KEY FACTS Catholics and most other Christians believe that sex before marriage and adultery are wrong because the Bible says so. Some Christians believe that sex before marriage can be accepted with certain conditions. Christians believe that marriage is for love and to raise a Christian family and should last for life.

MAIN FACTS

Sex outside marriage

Catholics and most other Christians believe that sex should only happen in marriage and so sex before marriage is wrong. They believe this because:

- the Bible teaches that fornication (sex before marriage) is wrong;
- Church leaders and the Catechism say that sex before marriage is a sin.

Some liberal Protestants believe sex before marriage is all right as long as the couple love each other, are in a long-term relationship and intend to marry eventually. They believe this because:

- Jesus taught that love is the most important thing;
- the Church has to come to terms with modern attitudes to cohabitation.

All Christians believe that adultery is wrong because it breaks the marriage vows and the seventh commandment.

Marriage

Christians regard marriage as a gift from God, but they do not have to marry. The reasons (purposes) for Christian marriage are:

- for a couple to be able to live together in love;
- for a couple to have lawful sex;
- for a couple to have comfort and companionship;
- for a couple to have children;
- for a couple to create a Christian family.

The main features of a Catholic wedding are:

- emphasis on marriage as a special sacrament so that God is a part of the marriage and marriage is for life;
- exchange of vows (promises) before God and witnesses;
- exchange of rings blessed by God;
- prayers, Bible readings on marriage, homily or talk on the duties of marriage;
- communion to unite the couple with Christ and each other.

Christian marriage is for life. As a vow (promise) in the marriage service says, 'to love and to cherish in sickness and in health till death parts us'.

3. You will need to know about divorce.

MAIN FACTS

As many as 1 in 3 marriages may end in divorce in the United Kingdom. There could be many reasons for the rise in divorces:

- It is easier and cheaper to divorce than it used to be.
- People live longer and have more leisure time so they spend a longer time together, which may make them bored with each other.
- Women are less prepared to put up with bad treatment from their husbands than they used to be.

The rise in the number of divorces means there are many more one-parent families, and many people think children need to be brought up by two parents.

Changes in jobs mean that people have to travel around the country more looking for work, which tends to break up the extended family. This means that parents have less help from relatives in bringing up their children.

Annulment	a declaration by the Church that a marriage never lawfully existed.
Divorce	the legal ending of a marriage.
Remarriage	marrying again after being divorced.

KEY WORDS

KEY FACTS

Divorce has risen in the UK, and up to 1 in 3 marriages ends in divorce. There are probably more divorces because society has changed and women are not prepared to be badly treated.

Remember couples can separate without getting divorced. A divorce is a legal declaration that a couple are no longer married and each of them is free to marry someone else.

4. You will need to know about Christianity and divorce.

MAIN FACTS

Catholics believe there can be no divorce because:

- Jesus banned divorce;
- when people marry, they make a covenant with God, which cannot be broken without God's consent. Therefore, a couple can never be divorced according to God's law.

Catholics do have Marriage Tribunals, which can decide that a marriage never existed (annulment), but there can be no divorce, and Catholics who have state divorces are not allowed to remarry in church.

Most Protestant and Orthodox Christians disapprove of divorce, but believe that if a marriage goes wrong and there is no chance of bringing the couple back together, then there can be divorce. They believe this because:

- God is always prepared to forgive sins if people are determined to live a new life;
- in the Gospel of St Matthew, Jesus allows divorce for adultery.

KEY FACTS

Christians have different attitudes to divorce:

- Catholics, and some other Christians, do not allow divorce because they believe the marriage vows cannot be broken.
- Most Protestant and Orthodox Christians disapprove of divorce but allow it if the marriage has broken down, because Christianity teaches forgiveness.

Marriage and Family Life

KEY WORDS

Nuclear family — mother, father and the children living as a unit.

Extended family — children, parents and grandparents/aunts/uncles living as a unit or very near to each other.

Reconstituted family — where two sets of children (step-brothers and step-sisters) become one family when their divorced parents marry each other.

5. You will need to know about family life.

KEY FACTS

Family life is the basis of society, but modern society has different types of families, any of which can bring up children.

MAIN FACTS

Family life has changed in the UK as attitudes to sex before marriage, cohabitation and divorce have changed.

- Changing attitudes to sex before marriage mean that there are many single-parent families where the mother is the only parent.
- Changing attitudes to cohabitation mean that in many families the mother and father are not married.
- Changing attitudes to divorce mean that many families are either single-parent (mother or father) or reconstituted families.

6. You will need to know about Catholics and family life.

MAIN FACTS

All Catholics believe that children should be brought up in a family with a mother and father (unless one of them has died). The New Testament and the Catholic Church teach that:

- parents should love their children and provide them with food, clothes, etc.;
- parents should set their children a good Christian example and encourage them to go to church and be confirmed;
- children should obey and respect their parents;
- children should look after their parents if they can no longer look after themselves.

Catholics believe that the family is important because:

- the Bible has many references to the importance of family life;
- Catholic marriage services refer to founding a family and bringing up children in a Christian environment as the major purpose of marriage;
- Catholics believe the family was created by God to keep society together;
- Catholics see the family as the basis of society.

How Catholic churches help with family life

- Catholic churches have infant baptism where parents dedicate their children to God and make promises about bringing them up in a loving Christian home.
- The Catholic Church runs schools which teach the National Curriculum in a Christian environment.
- Most Catholic churches run Children's Liturgies to help children learn about the Church and the Mass.
- Catholic churches provide classes for first communion and confirmation, which teach children about right and wrong.
- Catholic churches welcome families to Mass.
- Many Catholic churches run youth clubs and youth activities to keep children away from immoral activities.
- Catholic priests often act as marriage and family counsellors.
- The Catholic Church runs marriage and family guidance services (e.g. Catholic Marriage Care).

KEY FACTS

The Catholic Church teaches that the family is important because it is the basis of society, and having a family is the main purpose of marriage. Christian parents should look after their children and bring them up as Christians. Christian children should respect their parents and look after them when they are old. Churches should help parents with the upbringing of children.

Marriage and Family Life

7. You will need to know about Christianity and homosexuality.

KEY WORD

Homosexuality — sexual attraction to the same sex.

MAIN FACTS

There are three different Christian attitudes to homosexuality:

1. The Catholic attitude.

The Catholic Church teaches that homosexual feelings are not wrong, but homosexual sexual activity is wrong. The Church teaches that homosexuals should be celibate. The Church also teaches in the *Catechism* that it is very wrong to discriminate against homosexuals.

Catholics believe this because:

- it is the teaching of the Catholic *Catechism*;
- the Bible teaches that homosexual sexual activity is wrong;
- the Bible teaches that everyone should be treated with love and respect.

2. The evangelical Protestant attitude.

Many evangelical Protestants believe that homosexuality is a sin and that homosexuals should ask for God's help to become heterosexual. They believe this because:

- the Bible condemns all homosexuality and they believe the Bible is the word of God;
- they believe that being born again can save people from all sins including homosexuality.

3. The liberal Protestant attitude.

The Church of England and many liberal Protestants believe that life-long homosexual partnerships are acceptable, but homosexual priests should not engage in sexual activity. They believe this because:

- same sex relationships are not condemned in the Bible;
- the Bible passages on homosexuality need updating just like those on women and slaves;
- Christianity teaches love and acceptance; therefore homosexuals also should be loved and accepted.

Many doctors now believe that homosexuality is caused by genetics, and modern society disapproves of people discriminating against homosexuals.

KEY FACTS

The Catholic Church teaches there is nothing wrong with homosexual feelings or relationships as long as there are no sexual relationships. Evangelical Protestants believe that homosexuality is sinful. Liberal Protestants believe that homosexuality is acceptable as long as homosexual couples are in a life-long relationship.

Practice questions

(a) What is cohabitation? (2)

(b) Outline different Christian attitudes to homosexuality. (6)

(c) Explain why there are different attitudes among Christians to divorce. (8)

(d) 'Living together is better than getting married.' Do you agree? Give reasons for your opinion, showing you have considered another point of view. In your answer you should refer to Christianity. (4)

CHAPTER 4
SOCIAL HARMONY

1. You will need to know about the roles of men and women.

MAIN FACTS

A hundred years ago, women did not have many rights in Great Britain, but during the twentieth century women have gained:

- the right to vote;
- the right to equal pay;
- the right not to be discriminated against.

These changes have also changed the roles of men and women. In 1994, almost as many women as men were in paid jobs (but more of the women's jobs were part-time).

It is now accepted that men and women have equal rights and should both have the chance of a career. This also means that men and women have to share equally in running the home and bringing up the children.

| Equality | the state of everyone having equal rights regardless of gender/race/class. |
| Sexism | discriminating against people because of their gender (being male or female). |

KEY WORDS

KEY FACTS: Men and women now have equal rights in the United Kingdom. During the twentieth century, women gained the right to vote and to have equal pay to men.

2. You will need to know biblical teachings on the roles of men and women.

MAIN FACTS

Some of the Bible teaches that men are better than women and should have the main role in religion. The letters of St Paul teach that men are the head of women just like Christ is the head of the Church. They teach that women should not speak in church and should ask their husbands at home if they have any problems.

Other parts of the Bible seem to teach that men and women should have equal roles. *Genesis* says that God made male and female in his image. Jesus is shown as treating women as his equals and having women disciples who stayed with him at the cross and were the first to see him when he rose from the dead.

KEY FACTS: There are two types of teachings in the Bible about the roles of men and women. One teaches that men are better than women and should have the most important roles in religion. The other teaches that men and women are equal and should have equal roles.

Social Harmony 23

3. You will need to know about different Christian attitudes to the roles of men and women.

KEY FACTS

Catholics believe men and women are equal, but only men can become priests. Most evangelical Protestants and Orthodox Christians believe men are more important because of what the Bible says. Most other Protestants believe men and women have equal roles and have women priests.

Mary Magdalene was the first person to see Jesus after the resurrection.

Men and women are expected to share in the running of the home

MAIN FACTS

There are three different attitudes to the roles of men and women in Christianity:

1. The traditional attitude (held mainly by some evangelical Protestants).

This teaches that men should be the head of the family and women should not speak in church or be ministers/priests. The reasons for this view are:

- St Paul's statements in the Bible about women not being allowed to speak in church, and having to submit to their husbands;
- their belief that the Bible is the unalterable word of God.

2. The liberal attitude.

This teaches that men and women should have equal roles in life, including religion. Many Protestant Churches (e.g. Church of England, Methodist, URC) not only have equal roles for men and women, but also have women ministers/priests. They believe this because:

- St Paul said 'There is neither ... male nor female for you are all one person in Christ';
- Jesus treated women as his equals and had women followers like Martha and her sister Mary;
- Jesus' women followers were the only people to stay with him for his crucifixion and Mary Magdalene was the first to see him when he rose from the dead;
- they believe Jesus chose men as his apostles because of the culture of the time, not because of any theological reason.

3. The Catholic attitude.

This says that men and women should have equal roles and equal rights because men and women have equal status in the eyes of God. However, the Catholic Church teaches that only men can become priests. They believe this because:

- Jesus only chose men to be his successors;
- Jesus was a man and the priest represents Jesus in the Mass.

4. You will need to know about differences among Christians concerning the role of women in ministry.

MAIN FACTS

The Catholic Church teaches that men and women should have equal roles in ministry and so they have women eucharistic ministers, lectors, hospital and college chaplains, etc. However, they believe that women cannot be ordained as deacons, priests or bishops because:

- Jesus only chose men as apostles to be his successors;
- the women disciples of Jesus could perform many functions but were not at the Last Supper and were not his successors;
- Jesus was a man and the priest represents Jesus in the Mass. Therefore, priests have to be men.

Many evangelical Protestant Churches do not allow women to have any role in ministry because:

- Jesus only chose men to be his successors;
- St Paul teaches that women must be silent in church and that men should have all the roles in ministry.

Most Protestants give men and women totally equal roles in ministry and have women priests/ministers. They believe this because:

- St Paul said 'There is neither ... male nor female for you are all one person in Christ';
- Jesus treated women as his equals and had women followers like Martha and her sister Mary;
- Jesus' women followers were the only people to stay with him for his crucifixion and Mary Magdalene was the first to see him when he rose from the dead;
- they believe Jesus chose men as his apostles because of the culture of the time not because of any theological reason.

The section on the role of women in ministry is very similar to the section on the roles of men and women, but is focused on ministry and priesthood.

KEY FACTS

Catholics believe that women can have equal roles in all parts of ministry except the Mass and so women cannot be priests.

Many evangelical Protestants believe that women should have no role in ministry at all and expect women to be silent in church.

Most Protestants believe that men and women should have totally equal roles in ministry and they have women priests/ministers.

Social Harmony

5. You will need to know about multi-ethnic Britain and racial harmony.

KEY WORDS

Multi-ethnic society	many different races and cultures living together in one society.
Prejudice	believing some people are inferior or superior without even knowing them.
Discrimination	putting prejudice into practice and treating people less favourably because of their race/gender/colour/class.
Racial harmony	different races/colours living together happily.
Racism	the belief that some races are superior to others.

MAIN FACTS

Britain has always had immigrants, but after the Second World War, a shortage of workers led to many different cultures coming to Britain: Afro-Caribbean (Africans and West Indians), Indians, Pakistanis, Chinese, Bangladeshi. Even so, in the 1991 Census, only 4.8% of Britain's population came from ethnic minorities, and half of this 4.8% was born and educated in Britain.

In order to help with racial harmony, the Race Relations Act 1976 banned all forms of racial discrimination and any attempts to stir up racial hatred.

The benefits of multi-ethnic societies are:

- there is less chance of war, because people of different races and nationalities will get to know and like each other;
- there is more progress because new people will bring in new ideas and new ways of doing things;
- they are good for religion because it helps people to see there are many different races following a religion;
- they make life more interesting with a much greater variety of food, music, fashion and entertainment.

KEY FACTS

Britain is a multi-ethnic society where racial discrimination is banned. Multi-ethnic societies advance more quickly because they have more variety of ideas.

KEY FACTS

The Catholic Church teaches that racism is wrong because of the teachings of the Bible and the example of Jesus.

6. You will need to know about Catholic teachings promoting racial harmony.

MAIN FACTS

The Catholic Church teaches that all forms of racism are wrong and that Christians should work to bring about racial harmony. It teaches this because:

- Jesus treated people of different races equally;
- St Peter had a vision from God telling him that God has no favourites among the races;
- in the Parable of the Good Samaritan, Jesus showed that races who hated each other (as did the Jews and Samaritans) should love each other as neighbours;
- God created all races in his image;
- the Catholic Church has members, priests, bishops and cardinals of all races and colours.

Remember! The Catholic Church is worldwide and over a third of the world's population is Catholic. This means that more than half the Catholic Church is non-white.

Catholic Christianity Revision Guide

7. You will need to know about Martin Luther King and racial harmony.

MAIN FACTS

The work of Martin Luther King to promote racial harmony.

Martin Luther King was a young Baptist minister in Montgomery, Alabama, who led a peaceful protest when an old black woman was arrested for sitting on a bus seat reserved for white people. He then led marches and protests throughout America to make sure that black people were given equal rights. Although he was often arrested and persecuted, he would not let his followers use violence. In 1963 he led a civil rights march of 250,000 Americans of all races to Washington and made his speech about his dream of a world where all races and colours would be treated equally. He was awarded the Nobel Peace Prize for his work, but was assassinated by an opponent in 1968 when he was only 39.

The reasons why Martin Luther King fought for racial harmony.

Martin Luther King was influenced by the teachings of Gandhi on non-violence and how to overcome wrongs by the truth. However, his main influence was Christianity, especially:

- Jesus' teachings about non-violence and turning the other cheek in the Sermon on the Mount;
- the Parable of the Sheep and the Goats, which convinced King that God wanted all people to be treated as equals;
- the Parable of the Good Samaritan, in which Jesus showed that races who hated each other (as did the Jews and Samaritans) should love each other as neighbours;
- the teaching in *Genesis* that God created all races in his image.

> 'I have a dream that my four little children will one-day live in a nation where they will not be judged by the colour of their skin but by the content of their character.'
> Martin Luther King, Washington, August 1963

KEY FACTS

Martin Luther King was a black American Christian who fought for equal rights for black Americans using only peaceful methods. His work for racial harmony in the USA was based on his Christian beliefs.

Social Harmony

8. You will need to know about multi-faith Britain.

KEY WORDS

Multi-faith society	many different religions living together in one society.
Religious pluralism	when a society gives members of any religion the freedom and right to worship.
Religious freedom	accepting all religions as having an equal right to co-exist.

MAIN FACTS

Britain has had believers in different faiths for many years and all religions have equal rights.

As Britain became used to being a multi-faith society, people began to realise that it is possible to worship God and be a good person without being a Christian.

A multi-faith society has many benefits:

- It increases tolerance and understanding.
- It gives people an insight into different religions.
- It makes believers think seriously about their own beliefs.

However, a multi-faith society can cause problems for religion because:

- all faiths must be treated equally and not be discriminated against;
- religious people attempting to convert each other could be a form of discrimination: they are saying the members of the other faith are inferior because they need converting.

Some members and leaders of the different faiths in Britain do try to work together and show love and respect for each other. At official functions, leaders of all Britain's faith communities appear together and sometimes pray together.

KEY FACTS

Britain is a multi-faith society because several religions are practised in Britain and everyone is free to practise their religion.

If all religions are equal, no one religion can have all the truth.

Catholic Christianity Revision Guide

9. You will need to know about Christianity and other religions.

MAIN FACTS

All Christian Churches teach that there should be religious freedom – everyone should have the right to follow whatever religion they want. They also teach that people should not be discriminated against because of their religion. However, there are three different Christian attitudes to other religions:

1. Some Christians believe that Christianity is the only way to come to God and that all other religions are wrong.

They believe this because:

- Jesus said that he was the only way to God ('I am the way, the truth and the life. No-one comes to the Father except through me.' *John* 14:6)

2. Some Christians believe that people can come to God through different religions, but only Christianity has the full truth, and only Christians can be certain that they will go to heaven.

They believe this because:

- the Bible says that salvation (going to heaven) comes through believing in Jesus;
- although God can be found in other religions, the full truth about God can only be seen in his only son, Jesus.

3. Some Christians believe that all religions are equal and that they are just different ways of finding God. So each person should follow the religion they feel most at home with.

They believe this because:

- they do not regard the Bible as the word of God;
- they believe that God is a force, like gravity, which can be discovered by humans in different ways.

KEY FACTS

All Christians believe in religious freedom, but some Christians believe:

- Christianity is the only true religion;
- there is some truth in other religions, but Christianity has the whole truth;
- all religions are a path to God.

Practice questions

(a) What is a multi-faith society? (2)

(b) Outline Christian attitudes to the roles of men and women. (6)

(c) Explain how following Catholic teaching may help to prevent racism. (8)

(d) 'You should only marry someone from your own religion.' Do you agree? Give reasons for your opinion, showing you have considered another point of view. (4)

Social Harmony

CHAPTER 5
RELIGION AND THE MEDIA

1. You will need to know about the nature of religious broadcasts.

KEY FACTS

Religious broadcasts are programmes that the television companies claim as their religious output. They are specifically religious programmes, such as *Songs of Praise* and *The Heaven and Earth Show*.

Soaps with religious themes and sitcoms like *The Vicar of Dibley* are NOT religious broadcasts.

MAIN FACTS

When television broadcasting began, all channels were expected to transmit religious programmes on a Sunday, and the target audience was people who went to church regularly and accepted Christian beliefs.

As fewer people now go to church the target audience for most religious broadcasting is now 'the vaguely religious' (people who believe in God and a purpose in life, but who go to church only occasionally). However, there are still some programmes aimed at committed Christians and at committed members of other faiths for their religious festivals.

The Central Religious Advisory Council is a multi-faith body that advises television on religious broadcasts; they are not happy that the target audience has become 'the vaguely religious' and they want more worship programmes.

There is a considerable amount of religious broadcasting because:

- 85% of the population still claim to believe in God;
- more people attend Church than watch football matches;
- religious/moral issues often have a lot of general interest;
- just as television feels it has to serve the interests of those who like sports, etc., so it feels it has to serve the interests of the many people who like religion;
- television has a duty to inform the public of what is going on in important areas, and religion is an important area of life.

2. You will need to know about the variety of religious broadcasts.

MAIN FACTS

It is possible to identify certain types of specifically religious broadcasts, but these types often overlap.

Worship-type programmes

These are programmes which broadcast a service, have a lot of hymn singing or are mainly prayers and readings from religious books. The main programmes of this type are *Songs of Praise* on BBC1, and the Sunday service on ITV1. All the channels also have special worship-type programmes for Lent, Easter, Christmas, Ramadan, Diwali and Jewish New Year.

There are also several programmes on religious music, such as *Faith and Music*.

Magazine-type programmes

These show a mixture of news, reviews and interviews with people in the religious news. ITV networks *Sunday Morning* and has *Holy Smoke* on Sunday night. BBC1's main Sunday morning religious programme is *The Heaven and Earth Show*, which is like a religious daytime television magazine programme.

Religious documentaries

These are the most popular programmes, apart from *Songs of Praise*, and concentrate on religious and moral issues, which are investigated in a much deeper way than in the worship and magazine-type programmes. BBC1 had a regular religious documentary late on midweek evenings – *Everyman*. Channel 4 has a regular midweek religious documentary screened at primetime – *Witness*. The ITV companies often produce one-off religious documentary series. BBC2 often produces a series on particular religious issues, such as fundamentalism in different religions, or even on a particular religion, for example, *Living Islam*.

KEY FACTS KEY

There is a wide range of religious broadcasts on television, from the very religious worship-type programmes, such as *Songs of Praise*, to those dealing with religious issues in magazine-type programmes, such as *The Heaven and Earth Show*, and documentaries, such as *Witness*.

Religious broadcasts have a wide range of programmes to cater for all religious tastes.

Religion and the Media

3. You will need to know about one religious broadcast in detail.

Write an outline of the contents of the programme.

Explain why you think it had these contents.

Explain who would like it and why.

Explain who would not like it and why.

4. You will need to know about moral or religious issues in soap operas.

Religious and moral issues occur frequently in soap operas because they are a main feature of people's lives.

You should make a list of the religious issues dealt with in a number of soaps (very briefly). For example,

- *EastEnders* covered a religious issue when the vicar, Alex, began an affair with Kathy Beale.
- *Coronation Street* covered a religious issue when Roy and Hayley wanted to marry in church.
- *EastEnders* covered the moral and religious issue of euthanasia when Dot Cotton helped her friend, Ethel, to die.
- *Brookside* covered an incestuous relationship between a brother and sister.

KEY WORDS

Religious issue — something connected with the meaning of life or with a particular religious practice about which people argue, e.g. how to deal with someone dying, who should become priests, whether priests should marry, what you should do with your life.

Moral issue — something which is regarded as the right thing to do by some people and the wrong thing to do by others, e.g. divorce when you have a young family, racism, abortion, euthanasia.

5. You will need to know about one religious or moral issue in a soap opera.

MAIN FACTS

Refer to one religious issue you have watched in a soap and:

- name the soap;
- name the issue;
- name the main characters involved;
- describe how the issue was dealt with;
- explain why you think the soap dealt with this issue;
- identify other ways in which the issue could have been dealt with;
- explain how you would have dealt with the issue and why;
- explain whether you think a soap opera was a good way of dealing with the issue.

6. You will need to know about one religious theme in a film or television drama.

MAIN FACTS

Whichever film or TV drama you have watched, make a list of the following:

- The name of the film or television drama.
- The religious theme.
- Why the theme is important for Catholics.
- Why you think it was chosen.
- How the theme was dealt with in the film/drama.
- Whether you think this was a good way to deal with the theme. Remember to give your reasons.
- Whether the treatment was fair to religious people (use examples from the film/drama to show this), e.g. *Sister Act* was not fair to Catholics because the original convent worship was shown as typical Catholic worship when ...

Religion and the Media

KEY FACTS

It is very important that you think carefully about evaluation questions on the media. A question asking your views on a statement such as 'Religious programmes are boring' means that you should only look at religious programmes (worship programmes, magazine programmes and religious documentaries). YOU MUST NOT use soaps, films or any other television programmes.

Questions which refer to religion on television or in the media mean that you can write about all types of programmes that have anything to do with religion.

In any evaluation question, you must use examples from specific programmes/films to back up the points you make.

7. You will need to know about answering evaluation questions on religion and the media.

Practice questions

(a) Describe a religious theme or themes shown in a film or television drama series. (4)

(b) Explain how the theme was dealt with and whether it was effective. (8)

(c) 'Television soaps offer a good way of dealing with religious and moral issues.' Do you agree? Give reasons for your opinion, showing you have considered another point of view. (8)

CHAPTER 6
RELIGION: WEALTH AND POVERTY

1. You will need to know about the need for development.

MAIN FACTS

In the world today, there are developed countries, like Britain and Japan; developing countries, like Brazil and Malaysia; and less economically developed countries (LEDCs), like Bangladesh and Mali, where people regularly starve to death. If there is to be a fair world, then the LEDCs need greater help from the developed countries. It is also in the interests of developed countries to help the less developed because they need new markets for their goods and they need products like cotton, tea and coffee from the less developed countries. The world is now interdependent (we all rely on each other).

KEY FACTS

The world needs Less Economically Developed Countries (LEDCs) to develop so that they can buy goods from the developed countries, otherwise no one's life will improve.

2. You will need to know about the causes of world poverty.

MAIN FACTS

1. Most LEDCs are in areas where there are regular NATURAL DISASTERS like earthquakes and floods; for example, Bangladesh has bad floods almost every year.

2. Many LEDCs suffer from WARS sometimes caused by corruption, or by the way the country was split up when colonised by Europeans 100 years ago. A neighbouring country can often move from developing to less developed when war refugees arrive needing shelter, food, etc.

3. All LEDCs suffer from DEBT. They have to borrow money from developed countries' banks and pay large amounts of interest to the bank, which they could have spent on development.

4. Many LEDCs try to get money from abroad by growing and selling CASH CROPS (cotton, tea, coffee, etc.). The land used to grow these is often the best farmland, which could have been used to grow food for the starving people of the country.

5. There are also problems of health, too many children, lack of education, etc., which prevent the country from developing.

KEY FACTS

The main causes of world poverty are:
- natural disasters;
- wars;
- debt;
- lack of education;
- too many children;
- lack of investment.

Many LEDCs are paying 80% of their income on interest payments to banks in developed countries.

Religion: Wealth and Poverty   35

3. You will need to know about Christianity and wealth and poverty.

> **KEY FACTS**
>
> Christians believe that wealth is dangerous and may lead people away from God. Jesus taught in parables, such as the Parable of the Sheep and the Goats and the Parable of the Good Samaritan, that Christians have a duty to help the poor.

The love of money makes people do evil things, according to the Bible.

MAIN FACTS

On wealth

The New Testament teaches that wealth can be very dangerous – it is easy to worship wealth and material success instead of God. Jesus said that it is very hard for rich people to enter heaven. St Paul said that the love of money is the root of all kinds of evil. The Churches teach that Christians should earn money in only lawful and moral ways.

On poverty

Wealth should be shared and used to help those less fortunate. Jesus taught this in many parables, especially in the Parable of the Sheep and the Goats where he said that if Christians feed the hungry, clothe the naked and visit the sick and imprisoned, they are actually helping Jesus himself.

All of the Christian Churches today follow the teachings of the New Testament that it is a Christian's duty to help people in need, whether at home or abroad, because everyone is a neighbour. Jesus said in the Parable of the Good Samaritan that Christians must love their neighbours whatever their race or country.

4. You will need to know about the work of one religious agency to relieve world poverty.

MAIN FACTS

CAFOD was founded by the Catholic Churches of England and Wales to help relieve poverty outside Britain. Its aim is to help people to help themselves so that they do not need aid in the future. It mainly works through groups of Christians who live in the country concerned and so know the problems and the best way to deal with them. This also means that CAFOD can make sure all the aid gets where it is intended.

CAFOD:

- raises funds in Britain through the Catholic churches and also through Family Fast Days in Lent and October;
- provides aid for emergencies such as floods, earthquakes and wars;
- provides long-term aid to help countries develop, for example, helping the six million street children of Brazil through 'The Community Taking Reponsibility for its Children' and helping the Hola Catholic Mission in Kenya to develop a health programme with the subsistence nomads;
- educates Catholics in Britain so that they realise why there is a need for Catholics in Britain to raise funds for and help Christians in the developing world.

How CAFOD tries to remove the causes of world poverty

Natural disasters	CAFOD sends emergency supplies to deal with the effects of earthquakes, floods, volcanoes, etc.
Wars	CAFOD works with the United Nations and other groups trying to bring peace.
Debt	CAFOD was one of the leaders of Jubilee 2000 trying to persuade world leaders to cancel the debts of LEDCs.
Cash crops	CAFOD helps LEDCs to get a fair price for their crops.
Education	CAFOD funds schools and teachers in LEDCs.
Health	CAFOD helps to set up clinics and hospitals. It also works to provide clean water and health advice.
Lack of food	CAFOD is providing training in new farming methods and ways of preventing desertification, etc.

KEY FACTS

CAFOD was founded by the Catholic Churches in England and Wales to help LEDCs and remove the causes of world poverty. It raises funds in Britain to financially support Christians in LEDCs who are working to develop their countries; for example, it helps the Hola Catholic Mission in Kenya to develop a health programme with the subsistence nomads.

Jubilee 2000 is a campaign begun by groups like CAFOD who were inspired by the Bible to get the governments and banks of the developed world to cancel LEDC debts.

Religion: Wealth and Poverty

5. You will need to know about the work of one Catholic organisation to relieve poverty and suffering in the UK.

KEY FACTS

The Vincent de Paul Society is a Catholic organisation which tries to relieve poverty in the UK by collecting from rich Catholic parishes and using the money to help the homeless and poor in the inner cities of the UK.

MAIN FACTS

Every Catholic diocese in England and Wales is involved in helping to relieve poverty and suffering in the UK through its social care committee. Most parishes have a branch of the St Vincent de Paul Society, which is dedicated to helping the poor in the United Kingdom. They collect funds and clothes from rich parishes and then organise soup runs and shelters for the homeless in the inner cities.

Their work is based on Jesus' Parable of the Rich Man and Lazarus and all the Catholic teachings on helping the poor as a way of loving your neighbour.

Practice questions

(a) Outline the causes of world poverty. (4)

(b) Explain how one Catholic agency is trying to remove the causes of world poverty. (8)

(c) 'Only religious organisations can solve world poverty.' Do you agree? Give reasons for your opinion, showing that you have considered another point of view. (8)

GOOD ANSWERS TO EXAM QUESTIONS FOR CHAPTERS 1–6

Believing in God

(a) What is a miracle? (2)

An event which can only be explained as an act of God.

(b) Describe a religious experience. (6)

A religious experience occurred when I was in hospital in Austria. I had had a bad accident and I remember seeing everything that I had done flash before me. The problem was that I was myself and yet I didn't feel as though I was myself. I remember the lights growing dim and I felt as though I was at one with the world. It was very calm and peaceful and I remember everything turning hazy and it was also unclear. I felt I was with God. A religious experience often seems unnatural and it is something personal to you, but you feel God is real.

(c) Explain how Catholics respond to the problem of evil and suffering. (8)

Catholics respond to the problem of evil and suffering in several ways. The main way is through trying to get rid of evil and suffering. So, Catholics pray for those who suffer and try to help them. They do this because of the example and teaching of Jesus, which shows that Catholics must try to get rid of evil and help people who are suffering. Catholics also try to explain how God can be good and all-powerful and still allow evil and suffering to exist. One way they do this is to claim that humans were given free will by God to prepare their souls for heaven. This means that evil and suffering is the fault of humans misusing their free will, not the fault of God. Many Catholics also respond by saying they do not know why there is evil and suffering, but God must have his reasons.

(d) 'No one can be sure that God exists.' Do you agree? Give reasons for your opinion, showing you have considered another point of view. (4)

Some people might disagree with this statement because they are Christians who are sure that God exists. They believe this because they believe the Bible is a book written by God and so God must exist. They may also be sure because of their own religious experiences, such as praying for someone who has cancer and their being cured. This makes them sure that God exists because he answered their prayers.

However, I think they are wrong and I would agree with this statement. There is no evidence that the Bible came from God and their friend might have recovered anyway. I think there is no scientific evidence that God exists, and things such as evil and suffering make it seem that there can be no God, because if I were God, I would not let such things happen. So I agree with this statement.

Matters of Life and Death

(a) What is immortality? (2)

The idea that the soul lives on after the death of the body.

(b) Outline Christian attitudes to euthanasia. (6)

All Christians are against euthanasia because they believe that life is sacred and belongs to God. To end someone's life to give them an easy death is the same as murder, which is banned by the sixth commandment. However, Christians have different attitudes about life-support machines. Some Christians think they can be switched off when people are braindead, but others think they cannot. Most Christians believe that doctors can give drugs to relieve the pain of terminally ill patients even though it will shorten their lives.

(c) Explain why there are different beliefs among Christians about life after death. (8)

Catholics believe that when people die, if they are pure Christians they will go to heaven; if they are Christians with unforgiven sins or good members of other faiths, they will go to purgatory, where they will have the chance to atone for their sins, then, on the Last Day, they will go to heaven. Evil people will go to hell. Catholics believe this because it is the teaching of the Church, based on the Bible.

Other Christians believe in the immortality of the soul. This means that when you die, your soul lives on and goes to heaven or hell straight away. They believe this because of the sayings of Jesus for example, like when he told the robber on the cross with him that he would go to paradise that day. Some believe it because they believe in ghosts.

So there are different beliefs because there are different attitudes to the authority of the Church. Also Christians interpret the Bible in different ways and have different experiences of life.

(d) 'Religious people should never have an abortion.' Do you agree? Give reasons for your opinion, showing you have considered another point of view. (4)

I can see why people might say this because most religions say that you should not have abortions. For example, Catholics say that abortion is like murder, it is breaking one of the Ten Commandments and you must not have an abortion. The Catholic Church teaches that life begins at the moment of conception and that to abort a foetus is, therefore, to take a life that God has given and is consequently sinful and wrong.

However, this ignores the evidence from other religions. Islam allows an abortion if the mother's life is in danger. Protestant Christians also allow an abortion if the mother's life is at risk or if the child is a result of rape. So, if there are situations when some religions allow abortion, it can't be true to say that religious people should never have abortions. So even though I agree with the Catholic view about abortion, I think the statement is wrong because there are non-Catholic religious people who allow abortion in some circumstances.

Marriage and Family Life

(a) What is cohabitation ? (2)

Living together without being married.

(b) Outline different Christian attitudes to homosexuality. (6)

There are three different Christian attitudes to homosexuality. The Catholic Church teaches that homosexual feelings are not wrong, but homosexual sexual activity is wrong. The Church teaches that homosexuals should be celibate. The Church also teaches in the *Catechism* that it is very wrong to discriminate against homosexuals. Many evangelical Protestants believe that homosexuality is a sin and that homosexuals should ask for God's help to become heterosexual. The Church of England and many liberal Protestants believe that lifelong homosexual partnerships are acceptable, but homosexual priests should not engage in sexual activity.

(c) Explain why there are different attitudes among Christians to divorce. (8)

Christians have different views about divorce because some Christians allow divorce and some (mainly Catholics) don't allow it. Some Christians don't allow divorce because in the marriage service, you promise to stay with your partner until death parts you, and this promise is made to God, so only God can end the marriage. Also Jesus said that divorce had been allowed by Moses, but he thought it was wrong.

Other Christians allow divorce because they believe that Christianity is all about forgiveness and being allowed a second chance by God, so they think people should be allowed to divorce if their marriage has collapsed. They also point to a saying of Jesus that allowed divorce in the case of adultery.

(d) 'Living together is better than getting married.' Do you agree? Give reasons for your opinion, showing you have considered another point of view. In you answer you should refer to Christianity. (4)

I can see why some people might say this. They might look at the high divorce rate and the cost of getting divorced and say that you might just as well live together and it will then be easier if you break up.

However, I do not agree because no religious person can agree with this. Christianity teaches that if you are in love with someone and want to live with them and have children, you must get married. Catholics are taught that sex should only occur inside marriage and I think this is good because it means that if a child results from sex it will be brought up properly. It must also be the case that it is more stable to be married and it is a better environment for children. After all, if 1 in 4 marriages fail, that means 3 in 4 succeed, and I don't think living together will have such a high success rate. Therefore, I disagree with the statement.

Social Harmony

(a) What is a multi-faith society? (2)

A multi-faith society is one where people from different backgrounds, religions and beliefs are living in the same area.

(b) Outline Christian attitudes to the roles of men and women. (6)

There are three different attitudes to the roles of men and women in Christianity. The traditional attitude (held mainly by some evangelical Protestants) teaches that men should be the head of the family and women should not speak in church or be ministers/priests. The liberal attitude teaches that men and women should have equal roles in life including religion. Many Protestant Churches (e.g. Church of England, Methodist, URC) not only have equal roles for men and women, but also have women ministers/priests. The Catholic attitude is that men and women should have equal roles and equal rights because men and women have equal status in the eyes of God.

(c) Explain how following Catholic teaching may help to prevent racism. (8)

Catholics say God loves anyone of any race and colour because he made everyone, and following this teaching should stop racism. The story of the Good Samaritan teaches Catholics that they should not be racist. The story goes something like, a man was robbed on a road and needed help. A priest walked past without helping, so did a second Jewish religious leader, but the third, a Samaritan, helped the Jew even though the two races didn't like each other. Christians should follow the teaching of Jesus and behave like the Samaritan who was not racist and this may help to prevent racism.

Catholics also believe in loving their neighbour, which means they can't be racist. Also the Catholic *Catechism* says racism is wrong and that Catholics must not be racist. So following Catholic teachings should help to prevent racism.

(d) 'You should only marry someone from your own religion.' Do you agree? Give reasons for your opinion, showing you have considered another point of view. (4)

No I don't agree with this statement, although I can see a couple of reasons why this might be said. The reasons why I don't agree are that everyone has the right to marry who they want and at the end of the day all religions worship the same God, don't they? I mean they might have different ways of worshipping, but it is the same God.

I think some people might agree because some religions don't want to pollute themselves with having other religions in them. Also problems arise such as when a Muslim girl marries a Catholic man, which religion will the children follow? Even so, I think you should have the choice and I'm sure it can work if you really love each other. Therefore, I think the statement is wrong and I disagree with it.

Religion and the Media

(a) Describe a religious theme or themes shown in a film or television drama series. (4)

In *Four Weddings and a Funeral* there are several religious themes, but especially as the title says, weddings and funerals. The weddings are in church and there is a religious theme because there is some investigation of what a religious marriage is about. The funeral deals not only with the religious aspect of a funeral, but also the meaning of life, which is a very religious theme.

(b) Explain how the theme was dealt with and whether it was effective. (8)

I watched *Four Weddings and a Funeral* before we did it in RE and I never really thought of it as a religious film, but now that we have watched it and discussed it, I think it dealt with the two religious themes very well.

The film is about Charles, a young single man, who keeps getting invited to weddings. At the first wedding he is the best man and loses the wedding rings. However, the service is shown almost in full, with a clear account of the purposes of Christian marriage and the commitment involved in the vows. At this first wedding Charles met an American woman, Carrie, and fell in love with her, but did nothing about it.

The second wedding showed the humour of a learner priest taking a wedding, but also the way people make church weddings a social rather than a religious occasion.

The third wedding was a Scottish one and showed how Carrie was marrying for money and security rather than love.

The fourth wedding didn't actually take place because Charles was marrying someone he didn't love because he thought he ought to be married the same as all his friends, but the words of the service and the appearance of Carrie made him stop the wedding. These four weddings showed that a Church wedding should be a serious lifelong commitment for love.

A major figure at the first three weddings was Gareth, a gay older man. He had a heart attack at the third wedding and his funeral was very sad. The way it was dealt with showed that we need religious services to cope with death and that funerals give us a chance to think about the meaning of life.

(c) 'Television soaps offer a good way of dealing with religious and moral issues.' Do you agree? Give reasons for your opinion, showing you have considered another point of view. (8)

Some people might disagree because if a person wants help, the character or situation in the soap might provoke a wrong decision so that the person makes the same wrong decision. And besides, TV soaps are made up, although some people think they are real, and so the situations are not really real. They could also upset or put pressure on someone who has been in a similar position to those of the character on TV. For example, someone having an abortion in a soap might upset someone who has had one in real life.

However, I do not agree with them. Programmes like *EastEnders*, *Coronation Street* and *Emmerdale* all deal with religious and moral issues. *EastEnders* had a good storyline when Dot Cotton was asked to help her friend Ethel to die. Dot was a Christian and the story showed how her religious beliefs conflicted with her love for her friend. I found this storyline very moving and understood more about why euthanasia is an issue for Christians much better after watching this than from reading the textbook on Christianity and euthanasia.

Coronation Street has adultery and *Emmerdale* has abortion, murder, under-age sex and sex outside marriage. These three soaps alone cover a wide variety of moral issues. *Coronation Street* once had Shamir, Deirdre's husband, murdered in a racist attack, which brought up racism.

Soaps also show how people deal with these problems so they actually help people get through their problems. For example, someone being racially abused can see how a character on TV deals with a similar problem, etc. My class has learned a lot more about moral issues through watching soaps in RE than we have in our PSHE lessons. Therefore, I agree with the statement.

Religion: Wealth and Poverty

(a) Outline the causes of world poverty. (4)

Natural disasters (e.g. floods, hurricanes and earthquakes) are a big cause of world poverty. Another cause is wars, which result in refugees and cost a lot of money. There are also problems such as reliance on cash crops, overpopulation, lack of clean water and health care, and lack of education. But I think the main cause is debt. The less developed countries are paying lots of interest to the Western banks. If they could spend this money on development, it would make a big difference.

(b) Explain how one Catholic agency is trying to remove the causes of world development. (8)

CAFOD tries to help with natural disasters by sending emergency supplies to deal with earthquakes, floods and volcanic eruptions. They are working with the United Nations to try to bring world peace and they are active in places like Rwanda to bring warring tribes together by setting up football leagues. CAFOD was one of the main founders of Jubilee 2000, the campaign to end third world debt by persuading banks and governments to cancel debts.

As far as cash crops are concerned, CAFOD co-founded Traidcraft, which is trying to get a fair price for the products of LEDCs. CAFOD helps with the lack of education by funding schools in LEDCs and the problems of inadequate health care by funding clinics and hospitals. CAFOD has a well-building programme to solve the problems of unclean water and is working on appropriate technology to improve farming methods and reduce desertification so that LEDCs can produce sufficient food.

(c) 'Only religious organisations can solve world poverty.' Do you agree? Give reasons for your opinion, showing that you have considered another point of view. (8)

I can see why some people might agree that only religious organisations can solve the problem of world poverty. All religions teach specific things about wealth such as Christianity, which says that it should be shared with the poor, and Judaism, which says that the tithe should be used (one tenth of income given to the poor) to help the poverty-stricken individual to get help. The payment of the tithe in Judaism means that from an early age Jewish children are encouraged to put money into the pushka at home for people less fortunate than themselves. Groups such as CAFOD and Muslim Aid are working to solve world poverty.

However, poverty is helped not only by religious organisations, it is also helped by governments and charities who send aid to places that need it. Organisations such as Oxfam are often non-religious and they provide aid purely for humanitarian reasons. So it is not true that only religious organisations can solve world poverty.

Also the problems are too big to be solved by religious organisations. The debt of LEDCs causes many problems through interest payments and these problems can be solved only by banks and governments. Another reason for thinking that religious organisations are not the only ones who can solve world poverty is because of their attitude to wealth. If, for example, Christians say we should share our wealth, why are our churches so ornately decorated? This does not make sense and it is almost as if the Church is being hypocritical. Ornaments and decorations do not mean that it is easier to pray somewhere, they just mean that the church is nicer and more ornate to look at.

So I disagree with this statement and feel that only the governments have enough money to really solve the problem.

CHAPTER 7
BELIEFS AND VALUES

1. You will need to know Christian beliefs about the nature of God.

KEY WORDS

Unity	God's way of being one.
Trinity	the belief that God is three in one.
Monotheism	belief in one God.

KEY FACTS

Christians believe that there is only one God. They believe that the one God is experienced by Christians in three ways (Father, Son and Holy Spirit). This belief that God is one in three and three in one is called the Trinity.

MAIN FACTS

Christians believe in one God who shows himself to the world in three ways. This is the belief in the Trinity. This is often described as the great mystery of God being three in one. It is explained by the words **person and substance**: there is only one substance, God, but the substance reveals itself in three persons, Father, Son and Holy Spirit.

- Christians experience the fatherhood, power and creativity of God through the Father.
- They experience the love of God through the Son.
- They experience the presence, peace and purity of God through the Spirit.

However, the three persons are still only one God. The *Catechism* calls the Trinity the mystery of God.

2. You will need to know Christian beliefs about God the Father.

MAIN FACTS

The first person of the Trinity is God the Father. The main Catholic beliefs about God the Father are:

- *Luke* 11: 1–4, the Lord's Prayer, teaches that God is Christians' Father in heaven. God is holy and what he wants happens in heaven. It is the duty of Christians to ensure that what God wants also happens on earth. The role of God as Father means he will provide food and forgiveness for those who pray and live properly. The prayer for God to deliver from evil and not lead into temptation implies that God the Father is all-powerful.

- God the Father is God the Almighty Creator. Christians believe that God is a good creator – 'God saw all that he had made, and it was very good'. They also believe that God is all-powerful and can make anything happen.

Christians have different beliefs about the creation.

1. **Some Christians** believe that God created the universe and humans in six days as it says in *Genesis* 1: 1–2: 3:

- Day 1: the light to separate day from night.
- Day 2: the sky to separate the waters.
- Day 3: dry land and seas, vegetation (plants and trees).
- Day 4: sun, moon and stars.
- Day 5: fish and birds.
- Day 6: animals, creeping things, humans.
- Day 7: God rested and declared the seventh day a holy day.

2. **Other Christians** believe that God created the universe and humans in the way science says. They believe that God created the matter of the universe. Then about 15 billion years ago God chose just the right micro-second to explode the matter of the universe (the Big Bang). After the explosion, scientific forces such as gravity compressed the exploded matter into stars and solar systems. As part of this process our solar system was formed about 5 billion years ago. They believe that God caused chemical reactions on the earth so that life forms began and the process of evolution led to the arrival of humans.

> **KEY FACTS KEY**
>
> Christians believe that God the Father is the Creator of everything. They believe God the Father is all-powerful, provides for his people and forgives those who repent. God the Father means that God cares for his creation and loves his

Beliefs and Values

3. You will need to know Christian beliefs about God the Son (Jesus).

KEY WORDS

Incarnation	The belief that God took human form in Jesus.
Virgin birth	Jesus was not conceived through sex.
Christ	the Messiah/the Anointed One.
Crucifixion	the Roman death penalty suffered by Jesus when he was nailed to the cross.
Resurrection	the body being brought back to life after death/Jesus being raised from the dead.

MAIN FACTS

The second person of the Trinity is Jesus. Christians' beliefs about Jesus are that:

- God became human in the person of Jesus Christ (God becoming human is called the incarnation) through the virgin birth, which means that Jesus had a human birth, but not a human conception. This is why Christians believe that Jesus was both man and God;
- Jesus was the Christ, the one anointed by God to show people the nature of God and how humans should live;
- Jesus was crucified as a way of removing the power of sin from the world and giving humans the opportunity of going to heaven;
- three days after Jesus died on the cross, he rose from the dead and forty days later ascended to heaven to be with the Father again. Christians believe that the resurrection is proof that Jesus was both man and God because only God could rise from the dead;
- Jesus will return at the end of the world, judge everyone and decide who will go to heaven and hell on the basis of his judgment;
- Jesus is the head of the Church.

KEY FACTS

Christians believe that God became human in Jesus, who showed humans what God is like. They believe that Jesus died and rose from the dead to save people from their sins and to give Christians the chance to go to heaven.

4. You will need to know Christian beliefs about God the Holy Spirit.

MAIN FACTS

The third person of the Trinity is the Holy Spirit. Christians believe that:

- the Holy Spirit purifies people from sin (as seen in the baptism service). This is why one of the symbols of the Holy Spirit is fire, which is used to purify metals;
- the Holy Spirit is the way in which God communicates with humans. This is why another symbol of the Holy Spirit is wind, which represents the hidden power of God. At the first Pentecost, the Holy Spirit came upon the disciples as fire and wind (*Acts* 2);
- it is the Spirit who inspired the Bible and who inspires Christians today;
- the Holy Spirit is the bringer of peace. In the Old Testament, a dove bringing back an olive branch to the ark was Noah's sign that God was at peace with the world. This is why one of the symbols of the Holy Spirit is the dove.

The gifts of the Spirit are faith, hope and love, though many modern Christians believe that the Spirit can give special gifts such as healing and speaking in tongues.

KEY WORDS

Fire	when used of the Holy Spirit it implies purifying power.
Wind	when used of the Holy Spirit it implies power.
Dove	when used of the Holy Spirit it implies peace.

KEY FACTS

Christians believe that the Holy Spirit is God's power in the world. The Holy Spirit is the way God makes contact with people today. The symbols of the Spirit are wind, fire and dove.

Beliefs and Values

5. You will need to know Christian beliefs about sin and salvation.

KEY WORDS

Repentance	the act of being sorry for wrongdoing and deciding not to do it again.
Faith	belief in something without total proof.
Forgiveness	to stop blaming someone and/or pardon them for what they have done wrong.
Reconciliation	bringing together people who were opposed to each other.

KEY FACTS

Christians believe that sin is what separates people from God. Salvation is what brings people back to God through forgiving their sins. Christians believe that salvation comes through faith in the power of Jesus to forgive sins. Catholics believe that the salvation of Jesus comes through the sacraments.

MAIN FACTS

Christians define 'sin' as going against God's will and believe that sin separates people from God. All humans commit sins and some Christians believe this is what is meant by being born in original sin. To remove the separation of sin, God sent Jesus to die to save people from the consequences of their sins. The death of Jesus removed the power of sin, and those who believe in Jesus and show their repentance are saved from their sins.

The way in which Jesus saves people from sin is what Christians mean by salvation. REPENTANCE means to recognise one's sins, be sorry for having committed them and be determined to lead a new life following Jesus and deciding never to commit those sins again. It is the repentance and FAITH (believing without total proof) in the power of Jesus to FORGIVE SINS (pardoning people for what they have done wrong) that bring salvation.

Catholics believe that the forgiveness of sins brings humans and God back together (reconciliation) and is brought about by:

- the sacrament of baptism;
- the sacrament of reconciliation (confession, penance and absolution);
- the celebration of the Mass.

The nature of sin and reconciliation are shown in the story of Zachaeus (*Luke* 19: 1–9), a sinful tax collector who had faith in Jesus, confessed his sins and was forgiven by Jesus. He showed his repentance by giving back to people the money which he had cheated from them.

6. You will need to know about Christian values.

MAIN FACTS

In *Mark* 12: 29–31 Jesus taught that the two greatest Christian values are love of God and love of neighbour. Jesus showed how Christians should love their neighbour in two parables.

Jesus told the Parable of the Good Samaritan (*Luke* 10: 25–37) to answer the question, 'Who is my neighbour?' It tells how a Jew was travelling from Jerusalem to Jericho when he was attacked by robbers and left half-dead. A Jewish priest passed by and did not help, and another Jewish religious person, a Levite, also passed by without helping. However, a Samaritan saw him and took him to an inn and took care of him. As Samaritans and Jews were bitter enemies and of different religions, this shows that Christians must love their neighbour by helping anyone in trouble no matter what their race or religion.

Jesus told the Parable of the Sheep and the Goats in *Matthew* 25: 31–46. It describes how, at the end of the world, Jesus will return and separate people into the good and the bad like a shepherd separates the sheep from the goats. The good will be sent to heaven because they fed Jesus when he was hungry, clothed him when he was naked, looked after him when he was a stranger, and visited him when he was sick and in prison. The good will not know when they did these things for Jesus, but Jesus will say, 'Whatever you did for the least of these brothers of mine, you did for me'. The evil will be sent to hell because they did not feed the hungry, clothe the naked, help the stranger, or visit the sick and those in prison. This shows that Christians must love God and their neighbour by helping those in need of help.

KEY FACTS KEY

The two great Christian values are love of God and love of neighbour. Christians believe that the way to love their neighbour is to help those in need, as Jesus showed in the Parable of the Sheep and the Goats and the Parable of the Good Samaritan.

Practice questions

(a) What is the meaning of the word 'Christ'? (2)

(b) State what Christians believe about repentance. (6)

(c) Explain why the love of God is important to Christians. (8)

(d) 'Christian beliefs are unbelievable.' Do you agree? Give reasons for your opinion, showing that you have considered another point of view. (4)

Beliefs and Values

CHAPTER 8
COMMUNITY AND TRADITION

1. You will need to know Catholic beliefs about the Church.

KEY WORDS

Faith	belief in something without total proof.
Holy	of or relating to God.
Catholic	universal or worldwide.
Apostolic	belief that the Church can only be understood in the light of the apostles who saw, heard, walked with Jesus.
Body of Christ	belief that the Church is Christ's body in the world.
Communion of saints	followers of Jesus, both living on earth now and those who have died, are united with each other.

MAIN FACTS

Catholics, and most other Christians, have the following beliefs about the nature of the Church:

- **The Church is the source of faith.** Catholic Christians believe that all Christian faith is to be found in the Bible and the Tradition, but it must be interpreted by the Church. The Bible is the word of God which records the life, teachings and death of Jesus and the beginnings of the Church. The Tradition is the oral (spoken not written) gospel of Jesus given to his apostles and passed on through the bishops in the apostolic succession. This is interpreted for each new age by the Church, and so the Church is the source of faith. Catholics can also find faith through the services and fellowship of their local parish church.

- **The Church is the means to salvation.** Catholics believe that salvation comes from God through the life and death of Jesus. However, the Church is the means to salvation because salvation comes through faith and taking the sacraments of the Church.

- **The Church is one.** All Christians believe that Jesus is the Son of God and saviour of the world. However, Christians are now divided for many reasons – Catholics are divided from other Christians because of their beliefs about the authority of the Pope; Protestants are divided from other Christians because of their attitude to the authority of the Bible; Orthodox Christians are divided from other Christians because of their attitudes to the liturgy and national patriarchs. Nevertheless, all Christians are united in their belief in the Apostles' Creed and the Nicene Creed and so in their beliefs about God and Jesus. They are also united in their belief that Christians must be baptised (though they are divided about whether this should be as infants or as believers).

- **The Church is holy.** Catholics believe that the Church is holy because it comes from God and God is at work in his Church.

- **The Church is catholic.** The Church is universal (catholic) because anyone can join the Church, whatever their race or previous belief. Also there are Christians all over the world.

- **The Church is apostolic.** Because the Church was founded by the apostle of Jesus, all Christians believe the Church is apostolic. The Church today teaches the same message about Jesus as the apostles taught. However, Catholics also believe that the authority Jesus gave to Peter has been passed on from Peter to the Popes and to the bishops and through them to priests (apostolic succession).

- **The Church is the body of Christ.** Catholics believe that the Church is the body of Christ on earth because the Church carries on the work of Jesus on earth. The Church is like the body doing the work of Jesus through individual Christians, and Jesus is the head, the one who gives directions and who is the source of all the beliefs and ideas. The Church is the way Jesus is still present in the world after his resurrection and ascension.

- **The Church is the communion of saints.** Christians believe that they have a shared life with both living and dead Christians and they have a special relationship with the very holy or good Christians who have died. Catholic Christians believe that those who have been declared saints and who are in heaven can pray for Christians on earth. This is why Catholics light candles for saints or ask saints to pray for them.

> *Church with a capital 'C' is the name given to the whole Christian community, whereas church with a small 'c' is the name given to a building where a local Christian community meets.*

KEY FACTS

Catholics believe that the Church is:

- holy, catholic and apostolic – it belongs to God, it is worldwide and it was founded by the Apostles of Jesus;
- where people can find faith through the salvation of the sacraments and the teachings of the Church;
- one because all Christians believe that Jesus is the Son of God and accept the creeds;
- the Body of Christ, which means the Church is Christ's presence in the world;
- the communion of saints, which means that living and dead Christians can share with and pray for each other.

Community and Tradition

2. You will need to know Christian beliefs about Christian Ministry.

MAIN FACTS

'Ministry' means service and all Christians are called to serve God. Catholics believe some people are called by God to the sacramental ministry. These are called 'ordained' because they have had the sacrament of holy orders. Other Christians are called the laity.

The ordained ministries. These are deacons, priests and bishops. Only priests and bishops can celebrate the Eucharist and only bishops can ordain deacons and priests.

- **Bishops** are priests who are in charge of a diocese and are responsible for all the churches and priests in that area. They are also responsible, with the other bishops, for the teachings of the whole Church. They can celebrate all the sacraments.
- **Priests** can celebrate all the sacraments except holy orders and are usually in charge of a parish.
- **Deacons** can only celebrate the sacrament of baptism but can take weddings and funerals without the Eucharist, and serve the Church in other ways.

The role of the laity. The Catholic Church believes that the laity are called to serve God in the world and to help the ordained in the running of the Church. The Church has some special lay ministries:

- **Eucharistic ministers** – lay people, specially trained, who can give out the bread and wine after it has been consecrated by a priest.
- **lectors** – lay people, men or women, allowed to read the Bible lessons in church.

KEY WORDS

Bishops	specially chosen priests with responsibility for all the churches in a diocese.
Priests	those called to be ordained as ministers of the Word of God and the sacraments.
Deacons	those called to receive the Holy Spirit to assist the bishops, especially in caring for those in need.
Laity	those who share the mission of the Church without being ordained.

People become ordained through the sacrament of holy orders.

KEY FACTS

'Ministry' means service and all Christians try to serve the Church. Some Christians feel called to serve by being ordained. Deacons are ordained but can only administer the sacrament of baptism; priests are ordained and can celebrate all the sacraments except holy orders; bishops are ordained and can celebrate all the sacraments and are in charge of a diocese. The laity are unordained Christians who serve the Church in their daily life and work.

3. You will need to know Catholic beliefs about the celibacy of the clergy.

MAIN FACTS

All Catholic priests have to be celibate (not married or sexually active) so that they can dedicate the whole of their lives to the service of God. The Catholic Church feels that if a man is called to give the whole of his life to God, he cannot have a part of his life which is given to someone else, for example, a wife. Christian husbands and wives have duties to love each other and share responsibilities for their children. That limits what they can do to promote the gospel and to live in service to others.

The Orthodox Church insists on celibacy for bishops, but not for priests, because they feel that a bishop has too many responsibilities to be married.

No other Christian Churches insist on celibacy, but some priests and ministers in other Churches decide voluntarily to be celibate to help them in their calling.

You will need to be able to argue about whether it is better for priests to be allowed to marry or remain celibate.

KEY WORD

Celibacy — living without engaging in any sexual activity.

KEY FACTS

Catholic priests have to be celibate so that they can give their whole lives to the Church. Other Christians allow their priests and ministers to marry.

Protestants often have ministers instead of priests who can be women and/or married.

Community and Tradition

4. You will need to know Christian beliefs about the ordination of women.

KEY WORD

Ordination — the sacrament of holy orders making someone a priest, deacon or bishop.

KEY FACTS KEY

The Catholic Church says that only men can become priests because Jesus and the apostles were men. Other Churches have women priests because they believe men and women should have equal roles and because Jesus had women disciples.

MAIN FACTS

The Catholic Church teaches that only men can be ordained. It teaches this because:

- Jesus chose men to be the apostles and the apostles chose men to succeed them; therefore the belief in the apostolic succession means that only men can be priests;
- the priest represents Jesus at the Eucharist;
- Jesus was a man so the priest must be a man.

However, the Catholic Church teaches that men and women are totally equal and Catholic women can be deacons, teachers in theological colleges, Eucharistic ministers and lectors.

The Church of England and most Protestant Churches have women priests because:

- they believe men and women were created in the image of God and so either can become a priest/minister;
- many women followed Jesus and it was the women disciples who stayed with Jesus at the crucifixion and who were the first to see him when he rose on Easter Day;
- they believe that the only reason Jesus appointed men as apostles was the culture of his time. If he had been appointing apostles today he would have appointed men and women.

Catholic Christianity Revision Guide

5. You will need to know Catholic beliefs about authority and Tradition.

MAIN FACTS

1. The Bible. This is not one book, but rather a library of books. It is divided into two parts:

- The **Old Testament**, written before the birth of Jesus, which contains law books, history books, the books of the Prophets and a variety of other books known as the Writings. These books are about God's laws, the way he chose and looked after the Jewish people as a means of bringing the rest of the world to worship him, and prophecies about the coming of the Messiah.

- The **New Testament**, written after the death of Jesus, which contains the Gospels of *Matthew, Mark, Luke* and *John*; the history book of *Acts*; letters written by some of the Apostles to early Christians and the *Revelation* of John (these books tell the story of Jesus' life and death, resurrection and teachings, the beginnings of the Christian Church and advice on how to live a Christian life).

The Bible is therefore important to Catholics because it is:

- a record of God's actions in history;
- it contains God's commands on how Christians should behave;
- it shows Christians what Jesus did on earth.

2. Authority and Tradition. The Catholic Church teaches that the Bible (usually called Sacred Scripture in the *Catechism*) has equal authority with the Apostolic Tradition, which is the teachings handed down by Jesus to his apostles and through them to the Pope and the bishops. For Catholics the Bible and the Tradition are the only two sources of authority. Catholics believe that the Bible and the Apostolic Tradition should be interpreted by the Pope and the bishops in the Church's *Magisterium*. Many Catholics rely on this interpretation being given to them by their parish priest in homilies and Bible study.

3. The role of the Papacy. Catholics believe that the Pope is the successor of St Peter (who was given special authority by Jesus) and he is responsible for appointing the cardinals and bishops. The Pope is the Bishop of Rome and lives in Vatican City, an independent state given to the Pope by Italy in the nineteenth century. The Pope organises the Church through the Curia. The Pope gives advice to Catholics through encyclicals.

KEY WORDS

Bible	the Holy Book of Christians with 66 books split into the Old and New Testament.
Magisterium	the Pope and the bishops interpreting the Bible and tradition for Catholics today.
Apostolic Succession	the belief that bishops and the Pope continue the mission Jesus gave to Peter and the apostles.
Papacy	the office of Pope.
Dogmas	the beliefs of the Catholic Church.

KEY FACTS

Catholics believe that the authority of the Church comes from the Bible, which they regard as the word of God, and the Tradition of the Apostles. These sources of authority are interpreted for Catholics by the Pope and the bishops in the *Magisterium* of the Church. Catholics believe the Pope has special authority because he is the successor of St Peter, chosen by the Holy Spirit to lead the Church.

The Magisterium *is the main authority for Catholics. Its teachings are found in the* Catechism.

Community and Tradition

7. You will need to know Christian beliefs about the Virgin Mary.

KEY FACTS KEY

Catholics believe that the Virgin Mary is the model of the Christian life because of her life of service to God. They believe she deserves special devotion because she was the mother of God, born without sin (immaculate conception).

Assumption = the Catholic belief that the Virgin Mary was taken up to heaven without dying.

MAIN FACTS

Catholics regard the Virgin Mary as a model of the Christian life (her life is an example for Catholics to follow) because:

- she agreed to bear God's Son;
- she served her son so he could save the world;
- she shared Christ's suffering by standing at the cross;
- she helped the beginning of the Church through her prayers.

Catholics believe that Mary is worthy of particular devotion because:

- she is the Mother of God because she gave birth to the second person of the Trinity;
- at the end of her life she was taken up to heaven (assumption) and in heaven she can pray for the souls of Christians on earth;
- Mary said in the Bible 'all generations will call me blessed'.

Practice questions

(a) What does the word 'celibacy' mean? (2)

(b) Outline the role of the laity in the Church. (6)

(c) Explain why Catholics regard Mary as the model of the Christian life. (8)

(d) 'Everybody should do what the Pope says.' Do you agree? Give reasons for your opinion, showing that you have considered another point of view. (4)

CHAPTER 9
WORSHIP AND CELEBRATION

1. You will need to know Christian beliefs about the sacraments.

MAIN FACTS

Sacraments are public actions by which Christians receive grace and feel God's love and power in their lives.

Catholic and Orthodox Christians have seven sacraments: baptism, confirmation, the Eucharist, reconciliation, anointing of the sick, holy orders, marriage.

Most Protestants have two sacraments: baptism and the Eucharist.

KEY FACTS

Sacraments are the ways by which Christians receive God's grace and power. Catholics believe in seven sacraments, most Protestants believe in only two.

The Salvation Army and Quakers do not have sacraments.

Worship and Celebration 59

2. You will need to know Christian beliefs about the sacraments of initiation.

KEY WORDS

Water	used in baptism as a sign of purification from sin.
Chrism	the oil used in baptism, confirmation and ordination.
Vows	solemn promises made to God.
Renewal of baptismal vows	the confirming and deepening of the promises made at baptism.

KEY FACTS

Initiation means becoming a part of the Church and Catholics believe that people have to be baptised to become members of the Church.

Catholic parents have infant baptism for their children, when they and the godparents make promises on behalf of the child and the child has its sins washed away in water and is given its Christian name.

When the child is old enough it is expected to renew its baptismal vows in the sacrament of confirmation. It will usually be anointed by the bishop to make it a full member of the Church.

Some Christians only have adult baptism as their sacrament of initiation.

MAIN FACTS

1. **Baptism** comes from a Greek word meaning bathed or totally washed. In Christianity, baptism is the sacrament by which someone becomes a member of the Church and so it is the Christian initiation ceremony. The origin of baptism for Christians is the baptism of Jesus, which marked a new beginning in his life when God declared him to be his Son and he received the Holy Spirit. The act of washing in baptism symbolises God's grace in the cleansing or forgiveness of sins and the presence of the Holy Spirit.

Most Christian Churches baptise the children of adult Christians and this is known as **infant baptism.** In the Catholic ceremony:

- parents and godparents promise to bring up the child in the Christian faith, renounce sin and profess their belief in God the Father, in Jesus Christ, his only Son, and in the Holy Spirit (these are called the baptismal vows made on behalf of the child);
- the priest baptises the child by pouring water on the child's head three times and reciting the words, 'I baptise you in the name of the Father, and of the Son, and of the Holy Spirit';
- the child is anointed with chrism;
- a candle is lit and given to someone from the child's family to symbolise that the child has received the light of Christ.

Catholics believe infant baptism is needed because:

- children of Christians have to be treated as Christians;
- it has been the practice of the Church for over 1,700 years;
- it symbolises the Christian birth of the child, gives the child a Christian name and sets the child on the path to a Christian life;
- it brings parents into the Church and helps them to bring up their children in the way they promised at their wedding.

Catholic Christianity Revision Guide

2. **Confirmation** is the second sacrament of initiation. It gives young people an opportunity to confirm for themselves the baptismal vows taken on their behalf when they were babies. The sacrament of confirmation completes or confirms the process of initiation into the Christian Church and is usually administered by a bishop.

In confirmation:

- young people are prepared in confirmation classes so that they understand what they are doing and what beliefs they are agreeing to;
- the bishop explains the meaning of confirmation;
- those to be confirmed renew their baptismal vows;
- the bishop prays for them and asks God to send his Holy Spirit on them to guide them in the Christian way of life;
- each confirmation candidate comes forward and is anointed by the bishop making the sign of the cross on their forehead with chrism, saying the words, 'Be sealed with the gift of the Holy Spirit'.

Some Christian Churches (especially the Baptist and Pentecostal Churches) do not practise infant baptism and so do not have confirmation. They practise believers' baptism because:

- they believe baptism is a sign of repentance of sin and a decision to lead a new life following the way of Jesus. Only the person concerned can repent of their sins and make the baptismal vows; they cannot be made on your behalf by someone else;
- they believe that only adult Christians are recorded as being baptised in the New Testament.

> *Believers' baptism = the practice of some Churches of only baptising adults.*

Worship and Celebration

3. You will need to know Christian beliefs about the Mass.

KEY WORDS

Penitential rite	the confession and absolution at the beginning of the Mass.
Liturgy of the Word	the Bible readings in the Mass.
Liturgy of the Eucharist	giving thanks and praise, and consecrating the bread and wine.
Rite of communion	receiving the Body and Blood of Jesus.
Real presence	the belief that Jesus is present in the bread and wine.
Transubstantiation	the belief that bread and wine become the Body and Blood of Jesus.
Tabernacle	a safe place in which is kept the Blessed Sacrament for those who are sick.

MAIN FACTS

The Mass began with the Last Supper Jesus had with his disciples, when he gave them bread and wine to eat and drink saying it was his Body and Blood and told them to do the same in remembrance of him.

1. Structure of the Mass

- The Penitential Rite where the congregation confess their sins and receive absolution.
- The Liturgy of the Word with readings from the Bible and a homily to learn more about the faith, and prayers of intercession to help others.
- The Liturgy of the Eucharist, which symbolises the sacrifice of the Mass in the people's gifts and the bread and wine. By the prayer of consecration offered by the priest, the bread and wine become the Body and Blood of Jesus.
- The Rite of Communion where the people exchange the peace and share the holy communion by receiving the consecrated hosts. Any remaining consecrated hosts are placed in the tabernacle.
- Concluding Rite where the priest blesses the people and sends them out into the world.

2. Why the Mass is important in the lives of Catholics

The Mass is important to Catholics because:

- it is a way of making their lives good again after sins;
- it is the way of gaining the power to fulfil God's will in their daily lives;
- it is an obligation to attend Mass on Sunday to fulfil the commandment to keep the Sabbath holy;
- it is a means of uniting them with Christ and other Catholics;
- it is the Catholic way of nourishing Christians through the Body and Blood of Jesus;
- it is a sacrament of love from God to Christians through the sacrifice of Jesus.

3. Different meanings of the Eucharist

The Eucharist began with the Last Supper Jesus had with his disciples, when he gave them bread and wine to eat and drink and said it was his Body and Blood and told them to do the same in remembrance of him. It was used by the early Christians and St Paul describes early Eucharists in his letter to the Corinthians. So, the Eucharist is the earliest recorded Christian worship.

- **Catholics** believe that in the Eucharist the inner substance of bread and wine is mysteriously changed into the Body and Blood of Jesus (transubstantiation). The Mass is a sacrifice, both remembering the sacrifice of Jesus and the sacrifice of the people when they promise to live a new life. The Eucharist unites people with God and with each other (communion) as the real presence of Christ enters the people in the bread and wine.

- **The Orthodox Christians** believe that the bread and wine are mysteriously changed into the Body and Blood of Jesus through the epiklesis prayer and the real presence of Christ enters the people in the bread and wine.

- **Most Protestants** believe that the elements (bread and wine) are not changed, they are symbols of Christ's spiritual presence. They believe the communion unites the people with each other and with God through the spiritual presence of Christ.

- **The Salvation Army and the Quakers** have no Eucharist because they believe that Jesus is the only priest, there is no need for rituals, and worship should be direct contact with God without symbols like bread and wine.

- **The Church of England** has some members who have the same beliefs about the Eucharist as Catholics and some who have the same beliefs as other Protestants.

KEY FACTS

The Mass is the main form of worship for Catholics. It involves confession of sins, readings from the Bible, and the Eucharist, where the priest consecrates the bread and wine so that the people can receive the Body and Blood of Jesus in the rite of communion. Catholics are expected to attend Mass every Sunday to keep the Sabbath holy.

Christians understand the Eucharist and communion in different ways: Catholics believe in transubstantiation where the bread and wine change their inner form to the Body and Blood of Jesus; most Protestants believe the bread and wine do not change, but that Jesus becomes spiritually present.

Many Protestant Churches have separate glasses for the communion and use grape juice rather than wine.

Worship and Celebration

4. You will need to know Christian beliefs about the sacraments of healing.

KEY WORDS

Contrition	a prayer or action that deepens sorrow for the sin and awareness of the consequences of sin.
Penance	an action showing contrition.
Absolution	through the action of the priest God grants pardon and peace.

KEY FACTS

Catholics believe that the sacrament of reconciliation (confession) heals people by forgiving their sins and bringing them back to God. The sacrament of the anointing of the sick heals people by giving them spiritual strength to face serious illness or death.

The sacrament of anointing the sick used to be called the 'last rites'.

MAIN FACTS

1. Penance and Reconciliation (confession)

In this sacrament, Catholics confess their sins to a priest and receive absolution. The main features of the sacrament are:

- contrition – the person confessing must be sorry for their sin and determined not to commit it again;
- confession – admitting responsibility to God through the priest;
- satisfaction – compensating anyone wronged and being prepared to make penance to God;
- absolution – the priest then gives absolution and an act of penance to be performed.

2. Anointing of the Sick

This sacrament gives strength to those who are seriously ill and near death. The main features of the sacrament are:

- the person receiving the sacrament confesses their sins (if possible);
- the priest anoints the forehead and hands of the person with chrism;
- the person is given communion (viaticum – food for the journey to heaven).

These sacraments are called sacraments of healing because:

- penance reconciles people with God and other people;
- penance brings peace to a troubled conscience;
- anointing gives spiritual strength and healing;
- anointing may help healing from a serious illness;
- anointing reconciles the person with God and the Christian community.

64   Catholic Christianity Revision Guide

5. You will need to know Christian beliefs about Advent and Christmas.

MAIN FACTS

Advent is a four week preparation for Christmas. Catholics see Advent as a time not only to reflect on the coming of Jesus at Christmas, but to prepare for his second coming at the end of the world and the Final Judgment.

Christmas celebrates the birth of Jesus and is based on the Bible stories of the Annunciation to the Virgin Mary by the angel Gabriel; Joseph being told by God that there was to be a virgin birth, the birth of Jesus in a stable in Bethlehem, the visit by the shepherds after the angels had told them of the birth of God's Son; and the visit of the wise men. The Bible also records the visit of Mary and Joseph to Bethlehem where Jesus was circumcised and where an old priest, Simeon, and a prophetess, Anna, recognised Jesus as God's Messiah.

Catholics celebrate Christmas with a Vigil Mass on Christmas Eve afternoon, Midnight Mass on Christmas Eve, a Mass at dawn and another later on Christmas Day. Christmas lasts for twelve days and there are special Masses for the Holy Family on the Sunday after Christmas and for the Virgin Mary on 1 January.

Christians believe that Christmas is so important because without the birth of Jesus there would be no Christianity and no salvation from sin. At Christmas God became man in Jesus (the incarnation) so humans could come back to God.

Advent — four weeks set apart to remember how God prepared people for the first coming of Jesus, and Jesus' promise that he will come again at the end of time.

Christmas — a festival of twelve days celebrating the birth and childhood of Jesus.

Advent is the four week preparation for Christmas, when Christians celebrate the birth of Jesus for twelve days. Christmas begins with a Vigil Mass on Christmas Eve and has special Masses for the Holy Family and the blessed Virgin Mary. Christmas is important for Christians because without the birth of Jesus there would be no Christianity and no salvation from sin.

Christmas ends on 5 January (Twelfth Night) because 6 January is the Feast of Epiphany

Worship and Celebration

6. You will need to know Christian beliefs about Lent and Holy Week.

KEY WORDS

Lent — 40 days set apart as a time of prayer, fasting and generous giving.

Holy Week — the week beginning with Palm Sunday, remembering events of the last week of Jesus' life.

KEY FACTS

Lent is 40 days of preparation for Easter beginning with Ash Wednesday. During Lent, Catholics give up things and meet with other Catholics to think about what it means to be a Christian today. Holy Week is the week before Easter when Catholics remember Jesus arriving in Jerusalem on Palm Sunday; the beginning of the Eucharist in the Last Supper on Holy (Maundy) Thursday; Jesus dying for the sins of the world on Good Friday.

MAIN FACTS

Lent prepares for Easter by remembering the way Jesus was tested by the Devil for 40 days in the desert. So for 40 days before Easter, Christians give up things (just as Jesus did in the desert), and on the first day of Lent (Ash Wednesday) they fast and confess their sins and have ashes smeared on the head as a sign of penitence. Many Catholics attend study groups at Church or in each other's homes to think about what it means to be a Christian today and to prepare for Easter.

Holy Week is the week before Easter in which Christians remember the last week of Jesus' life and especially how those events brought salvation to humanity. The main days are Palm Sunday, Holy (Maundy) Thursday and Good Friday.

Palm Sunday remembers the way Jesus was welcomed to Jerusalem by a crowd that, five days later, denied him. Catholics celebrate it by:

- processing near the church with palm leaves or branches;
- making a special entrance into the church;
- celebrating a special Mass with Bible readings of the events of Palm Sunday and Good Friday.

Holy (Maundy) Thursday remembers the Last Supper of Jesus with his apostles. Catholics celebrate it with:

- a special Mass when the priest washes people's feet as Jesus washed the apostles' feet;
- readings about the Last Supper and the arrest of Jesus;
- sufficient elements consecrated for Good Friday and Holy Saturday as no Eucharists are celebrated on those days;
- the altar stripped and all crosses covered, as Good Friday and Holy Saturday are days of mourning.

Good Friday remembers the death of Jesus. Catholics observe it with:

- a 3.00 p.m. service to mark the time of Jesus' death with Bible readings, veneration of the cross, and rite of communion using the hosts consecrated the previous night;
- prayers at the stations of the cross.

Holy Week reminds Christians of the salvation brought by Jesus' death and prepares for the joy of Easter.

Catholic Christianity Revision Guide

7. You will need to know Christian beliefs about Easter.

MAIN FACTS

Easter Day is the festival of joy as Christians celebrate the resurrection.

Catholics celebrate with the Easter Vigil which has:

- a ceremony of light to remember the darkness of the tomb and the joy and light of the resurrection;
- Bible readings to remember how the resurrection of Jesus brought back the goodness of the world at creation;
- renewal of baptismal vows to remember the rebirth brought by Easter;
- the Eucharist to remember that salvation now comes through the sacraments.

They also have a second Mass later in the day. Easter Day is the only occasion when Catholics are allowed to take communion twice in one day.

Christians celebrate on Easter Day because:

- Jesus rose from the dead and so must have been the Son of God;
- Jesus' resurrection completes the salvation from sin begun at the crucifixion;
- Jesus' resurrection means that those who believe in Jesus will also have eternal life as sin and death have been overcome.

KEY WORD

Easter — the festival celebrating the resurrection of Jesus.

KEY FACTS

Easter Day celebrates the resurrection of Jesus – Jesus rising from the dead on the Sunday after Good Friday. Catholics celebrate with the Easter Vigil when they renew their baptismal vows. It is the highlight of the Christian year because the resurrection gives Christians the hope of eternal life.

Easter eggs remember the new life of Jesus' resurrection.

Practice questions

(a) When does Lent begin? (2)

(b) Describe the ceremony of confirmation. (6)

(c) Explain the importance of the sacrament of reconciliation. (8)

(d) 'All babies should be baptised.' Do you agree? Give reasons for your opinion, showing that you have considered another point of view. (4)

Worship and Celebration

CHAPTER 10
LIVING THE CHRISTIAN LIFE

KEY WORDS

Service to others	gift of self, time and energy for the good of others.
Compassion	sharing the feelings and expressions of others.
Concern	to show compassion by becoming involved in other people's distress.
Justice	due allocation or reward and punishment, the maintenance of what is right.
Oppressed	all those who are denied.
Ten Commandments	the ten rules for living, given by God to Moses.

1. You will need to know Christian beliefs about the Ten Commandments.

MAIN FACTS

Christian values which are the basis for living the Christian life are found in the Ten Commandments and the Sermon on the Mount. Christians believe that the Ten Commandments were given by God to Moses, but they are commandments for Christians as well as Jews on how to live in the way God wants. Loving God is the first three commandments, loving your neighbour the other seven. The Commandments can be divided into:

Respect for God

Worship God alone

Do not misuse God's name

Keep the Sabbath day holy

Respect for others

Respect your father and mother

Do not kill

Do not commit adultery

Do not steal

Do not lie (bear false witness)

Do not desire (covet) your neighbour's wife

Do not desire other people's possessions

KEY FACTS

Christians believe the Ten Commandments were given to Moses by God to show people how to live. The first three commandments tell Christians how to treat God; the other seven tell Christians how to treat other people.

Remember! Love your neighbour is NOT one of the Ten Commandments.

Catholic Christianity Revision Guide

2. You will need to know Christian beliefs about the Sermon on the Mount.

MAIN FACTS

The Sermon on the Mount contains the main teachings of Jesus on how Christians should live. It contains the following:

1. Reinterpretation of the Law of Moses

- The Law said no murder, but Jesus said do not even become angry with your brother. Do not make offerings to God when you are quarrelling with your brother. Settle your arguments before you get to court.
- The Law said no adultery, but Jesus said do not even look at a member of the opposite sex with lust if you are married.
- The Law said only divorce if you have a certificate of divorce, but Jesus said do not divorce except in the case of adultery.
- The Law said do not break oaths made to God, but Jesus said do not take any oaths at all.
- The Law said an eye for an eye and a tooth for a tooth, but Jesus said if someone hits you on the right cheek offer them the left as well.
- The Law said love your neighbour and hate your enemy, but Jesus said love your enemies and pray for those who persecute you.

2. Displaying Religion

- Jesus said that when Christians give money to help the poor, they should do so secretly, so they are praised by God rather than humans.
- Jesus said that when Christians pray, they should pray at home directly to God, rather than standing on a street corner showing off their religion. He also said that prayers should be short and gave the example of the Lord's Prayer.
- In the same way when Christians fast, they should not let anyone but God know they are fasting.

3. Christians and Money

- Jesus said that it is impossible to serve two masters, so people cannot serve God and money. Christians must store up spiritual treasures not material ones.
- Christians should not worry about what is going to happen in the future. God looks after the birds and the flowers, how much more will he look after those who love him.

KEY WORDS

The Sermon on the Mount — Jesus' description of Christian living.

Displaying religion — making a show of your religion.

Judgment — the act of judging people and their actions.

The Golden Rule — the teaching of Jesus that you should treat others as you would like them to treat you.

KEY FACTS

The Sermon on the Mount is the teaching of Jesus on how Christians should live. Jesus reinterpreted the law of Moses to show that Christians should not divorce, should not get angry, should not take oaths and should love their enemies.

Jesus taught that Christians should not make a display of their religion, but should pray and fast and give charity secretly.

Jesus taught that Christians should not collect earthly treasures like money, but the spiritual treasures of God. Christians should not judge other people and should always treat other people in the way they would like to be treated (the Golden Rule).

Living the Christian Life

> *The Golden Rule is often said as 'Do as you would be done by'.*

4. Christians and Judgment

- Jesus said that Christians should not judge other people.
- Rather than looking at what is wrong with other people, Christians should first judge themselves and make themselves perfect.

5. The Golden Rule

Jesus said,

'So in everything, do to others what you would have them do to you, for this sums up the Law and the Prophets.' *Matthew* 7: 12

3. You will need to know about the expression of Christian values.

KEY FACTS

Christians should put their beliefs into action by service to others, compassion for those who suffer, concern for the cause of suffering, helping those in need, and by seeking justice for the oppressed.

> *Most Catholics show their service through helping CAFOD on fast days.*

© Jim Holmes/CAFOD

MAIN FACTS

Christians should put their beliefs into action. They can show their Christian values:

- **By service to others,** for example, by a job such as teaching or social work, or by doing voluntary work in youth groups, old people's lunch clubs, etc.

- **Through compassion for people who suffer,** for example, through work with homeless people, with the Red Cross, in nursing, by working with the hospice movement to help those with terminal diseases come to terms with death and to die surrounded by love.

- **In concern for the causes of suffering,** for example, by working for groups like CAFOD or by being involved in politics to remove the causes of suffering. The Jubilee 2000 Campaign was organised and run by a high proportion of Christians trying to persuade Western governments to cancel the debts of poor countries. The campaign drew inspiration from Biblical references.

- **By helping those in need.** Christian values expressed in such teachings of Jesus as the Parable of the Sheep and the Goats compel Christians to help those in need. Almost all Catholic churches have groups to help the poor and homeless and to support the work of CAFOD for suffering overseas, and have the St Vincent de Paul Society to help homeless people and drug addicts in the UK.

- **In seeking justice for the oppressed.** The Catholic Church in South America is working for justice for the street children of Brazil. The Christian Churches in South Africa worked for justice for black Africans by opposing apartheid.

4. You will need to know about two exemplary Christians.

MAIN FACTS

Mother Teresa was born in Yugoslavia in 1910. She took her vows as a Loreto nun at the Dublin headquarters when she was 18. She was sent to Calcutta as a teacher of Geography in the convent schools and whilst there she became concerned at the thousands of slum children who could not afford an education. In 1948 she founded a school for slum children in Calcutta. Then she found children dying on the streets and was given a disused Hindu temple to care for the dying. In 1950 she was given permission to found her own order of nuns, the Missionaries of Charity, and as Mother Superior she became known as Mother Teresa. The school and the home for the dying have since been extended to leprosy centres, other homes for the dying and other schools for slum children in African countries as well as India. In 1979 Mother Teresa was given the Nobel Peace Prize, which enabled her to extend the work of the missionaries.

Mother Teresa was inspired by the teachings of Jesus about caring for the homeless and the unloved, especially the Parable of the Sheep and the Goats and the Parable of the Good Samaritan. She herself said that working for the poor is like prayer and she always tried to work with Jesus and for Jesus in helping the poor.

Helder Camara was a Catholic priest in Brazil who originally thought all priests should support their government. Then, as Bishop of Rio, he became aware of the great extremes of wealth and poverty in Brazil. When he became Archbishop of Recife, he helped with the development of liberation theology, which through study of the gospels shows that Jesus called his disciples to liberate the poor. He struggled to get the Brazilian government to do something to help the poor. But he also opposed those priests who wanted to use violence to force the rich to do something. Camara believed in non-violence, and was responsible for a lot of initiatives by the Brazilian Catholic Church to help the poor.

Helder Camara was very influenced by Martin Luther King's ideas on non-violence and by the teachings of Jesus about wealth and poverty, especially Jesus' statement that he had come to bring good news to the poor.

KEY FACTS

Mother Teresa, the founder of the Missionaries of Charity, was an examplary Christian because she lived the Sermon on the Mount by helping poor children and caring for the homeless dying in India.

Helder Camara was an exemplary Christian because, as Archbishop of Recife, he worked to remove the oppression of the poor in Brazil by non-violent means.

Practice questions

(a) Name ONE of the Ten Commandments. (2)

(b) Give an outline of what Jesus said about displaying religion. (6)

(c) Explain why service to others is important to Christians. (8)

(d) 'It is easy to be a Christian today.' Do you agree? Give reasons for your opinion, showing that you have considered another point of view. (4)

Living the Christian Life

CHAPTER 11
A PLACE OF CATHOLIC WORSHIP

1. You will need to know about the architectural and other main features of a Catholic church or cathedral.

Remember to spell altar with two 'a's!

You must revise from the notes you made about the church or cathedral you visited. Remember to check that you made notes on the reasons for the features.

2. You will need to know about the role and function of the priest.

KEY FACTS KEY

The main functions of the priest are to administer the sacraments, represent Christ at the Mass and help the Catholics in the parish. The priest is important because only he can offer the Mass and release people from their sins.

MAIN FACTS

The main functions of the priest are to:

- administer the sacraments of baptism, marriage, reconciliation;
- represent Christ at the Mass and consecrate the bread and wine in the Eucharist, changing the substance to the body and blood of Jesus;
- prepare parents for the baptism of their children;
- prepare candidates for confirmation;
- prepare couples for marriage;
- conduct funerals;
- visit the sick and the bereaved (including taking communion to the sick);
- lead the Parish Council in the organisation of church finances and events;
- act as a governor for local Catholic schools and celebrate Mass there.

The priest is the most important person in the parish because:

- only he can offer the Mass, which all Catholics must attend at least once a week on Sundays;
- only he has the power to release people from their sins through the power given by Jesus to St Peter which is passed on through ordination;
- as someone ordained into holy orders, the priest brings Christ into the lives of the people;
- without the priest there can be no sacraments and the sacraments are the basis of Catholic Christianity.

Role and function = what a person or people do.

3. You will need to know about the role and function of the church in the parish.

MAIN FACTS

Many Christians would see the main role of the church to be a witness to God and Christ in the local community. Most churches fulfil this role by:

- providing the Mass and the sacraments for Catholics in the area;
- providing weddings, baptisms and funerals for those requiring them;
- providing Children's Liturgies so that children can learn about Christianity;
- providing confirmation classes for those wishing to be confirmed;
- providing opportunities for Christians to learn more about their faith, for example, discussion groups;
- providing social facilities such as youth clubs, mums and tots groups, lunch clubs;
- providing help for those in trouble, for example, through CAFOD and St Vincent de Paul;
- being involved in moral and social issues about which Christians are concerned.

The parish church is important because:

- without it Catholics would have no access to the Mass and the sacraments;
- it gives a sense of belonging to Catholics in the area;
- it is the main support for the local Catholic community;
- it is the source of Catholic life and faith in the area;
- it provides the help Catholics need to live a good Christian life.

KEY FACTS

The main role of the parish church is to witness for God and Christ in the area and to provide the Mass and the sacraments for local Catholics.

A Place of Catholic Worship

4. You will need to know about different forms and places of worship.

KEY FACTS

Christians have different forms of worship and different places of worship because of different beliefs. Catholics have worship based on the Mass which needs an altar and tabernacle. They worship like this because they believe the sacraments and Mass are the centre of the Christian life. Nonconformist Protestants have non-liturgical worship which needs a large pulpit and an open Bible on a table. They worship like this because they believe the Bible is at the centre of the Christian life.

Nonconformists are Protestant Christians such as Methodists and URC.

MAIN FACTS

There are differences in Christian forms of worship and places of worship because of differences in belief among Christians.

1. **Liturgical worship** is based on a set order of service such as the Mass. This is the only form of worship in Catholic and Orthodox churches and some Church of England churches. **Catholics** worship in this way because they believe that the Mass and the sacraments are the centre of life. The Mass has to follow a set form and has to be led by a priest to be effective. The sacrifice of the Mass requires an altar. Catholics believe statues are an aid to devotion and that the saints can take prayers to God. They believe that the Virgin Mary can pray for Christians on earth. Because they believe in transubstantiation, consecrated hosts are the body of Jesus and must be kept in a tabernacle. This means that Catholic churches have these features which are not found in Nonconformist Protestant churches: holy water stoop, statues of saints, statue of the Virgin Mary, statue of St Peter, a tabernacle, altar with candles, a crucifix, stations of the cross.

2. **Non-liturgical worship** is based on freedom of expression but with its focus on the Bible, a sermon explaining the Bible and prayers said without preparation. It is mainly found in Nonconformist **Protestant** churches and some Church of England churches. **Nonconformists** and some members of the Church of England believe that the Bible is the only source of faith and should be the centre of worship. They believe that all Christians are priests and that worship must fit the needs of the time. The Eucharist is not a sacrifice and there is only a spiritual presence of Jesus, so an altar is not needed. They follow the Ten Commandments in *Exodus*, which forbid the making of images, instead of those in *Deuteronomy*, which Catholics follow. This means that Protestant (mainly Nonconformist) churches have these features not found in Catholic churches: pulpit in the middle of the church; communion table instead of altar, with an open Bible on it; empty cross not crucifix; no statues or pictures.

3. **Charismatic worship** is similar to non-liturgical worship, but also has speaking in tongues, healing and gospel music. It is mainly found in Pentecostal and black churches. **Charismatics** believe that all Christians should be filled with the Holy Spirit and that worship should be based on the gifts of the Spirit, such as speaking in tongues and joyful worship. There are Catholic charismatics.

Catholic Christianity Revision Guide

Practice questions

(a) Describe the main features of a particular church or cathedral. (4)

(b) Explain why it has these features. (8)

(c) 'All Christians should worship together.' Do you agree? Give reasons for your opinion, showing that you have considered another point of view. (8)

CHAPTER 12
CHRISTIAN VOCATION

1. You will need to know about Christian vocation.

KEY FACTS

'Vocation' means calling from God. All Christians are called by God to follow Jesus and be good members of the Church. Most Christians carry out their call in their ordinary lives (daily life and work), but some Christians receive a call to be priests or monks or nuns.

MAIN FACTS

A vocation is a calling by God to a certain way of life. Christians believe they have been called by God to be followers of Jesus, to be members of the Church and to make their pilgrimage on earth. Sometimes God calls people directly by speaking to them and telling them what to do; more often people feel that God speaks to them indirectly through their experience of life or through natural or historical events. For example, Jesus heard the voice of God calling him when he was baptised by John, but someone like Mother Teresa felt God was calling her through her experiences of the dying in Calcutta and through the Parable of the Sheep and the Goats.

As well as the vocation of all Christians, there can also be a personal call by God to a specified state of life. A Christian can be called in many different ways. It is possible to be called to marriage, nursing, teaching, etc. However, traditionally a Christian vocation means being called by God either to be a priest or to join a religious order (this is often called the religious life and means becoming a monk or a nun).

2. You will need to know about Christian vocation and daily life.

MAIN FACTS

All Christians are called to be disciples of Jesus by following his example of love, service and compassion. They are also called to witness to their faith through their daily life and work so that by their example others may become Christians.

Most Christians fulfil their vocation to discipleship and witness in an ordinary life.

In their daily work (job) they:

- do their job to the best of their ability;
- do not cheat their employer or customers;
- are always honest and reliable.

In their daily life they:

- help anyone who needs help;
- are always honest and kind;
- show Christ's love to everyone they meet.

KEY FACTS KEY

Christian vocation can be carried out in an ordinary life. If Christians do their job to the best of their ability and in all their life help those who need help, are honest and reliable and show Christ's love to those they meet, they are following God's call.

Daily life and work = what you do in your job and your ordinary life.

Christian Vocation 77

3. You will need to know about religious communities.

KEY FACTS

A religious community is a group of Christians who have joined together to become perfect Christians. There are different types of religious communities, not just monks and nuns. Some lead an active life, others lead a contemplative life.

MAIN FACTS

Christians who have a vocation to the religious life join a religious community. Many religious communities are based in monasteries, which are communities of Christians who have separated themselves from worldly life to become as perfect Christians as possible.

Such people are known as monks or nuns and they live a special way of life known as 'a rule'. There are many types of religious communities (not all are monks and nuns). The Iona community in Scotland has men and women, Protestants and Catholics. The Corrymeela community in Northern Ireland is made up of Protestants and Catholics who feel called to live together and show that peace and reconciliation is possible in Northern Ireland.

Some communities follow **the contemplative life.** Contemplation is a state of mind focused on God. The contemplative is a person who seeks to live with a permanent awareness of God's presence. Contemplatives read and meditate on the Bible to understand God's purpose and to experience his love in their lives. They speak to God in prayer, but what God says to them is more important than what they say to God. By concentrating on prayer and meditation, contemplatives can serve others by praying for them and by becoming so close to God that they can show the world a bit more of what God is like. They believe this is the best way of loving God and loving their neighbour.

Other communities have a rule based on prayer and meditation but follow **the active life** rather than the contemplative life. Such monks and nuns usually teach or nurse or help the poor. They believe this is the best way of loving God and loving their neighbour.

You will need to be able to argue the benefits and drawbacks of both the contemplative and the active life.

5. You will need to know about the evangelical counsels.

MAIN FACTS

Although religious communities are based on different rules from different founders, they have certain things in common. They must all follow the evangelical counsels of poverty, chastity and obedience.

- Poverty is needed for complete dedication to God as Jesus showed when he told the rich young man to sell all he had so he could follow Jesus.
- Chastity is needed so that the religious can be totally devoted to God.
- Obedience is needed to follow the example of Jesus, who was totally obedient to God his Father, and for the efficient running of the community under the leadership of the Abbot/Mother Superior, etc.

KEY FACTS

The evangelical counsels are the vows of poverty, chastity and obedience that members of religious communities have to take.

Chastity = no sex.

6. You will need to know the purpose and practice of one religious community.

MAIN FACTS

The purpose of the Missionaries of Charity

The Missionaries of Charity are an order of nuns founded by Mother Teresa of Calcutta in 1950. Teresa was a Loreto nun working in India as a teacher. She wanted to do more for the poverty-stricken people of Calcutta who could lie dying in the streets with no one to care about them. The nuns have a centre in Calcutta (the Place of the Pure Heart) and run schools, hospices and leprosy centres in India and Africa.

The practice of the Missionaries of Charity

The order is centred on the Eucharist and prayer. Every day begins with Mass and meditation. There is more meditation and the Liturgy of the Hours from 12.30 to 2.00 p.m. and from 6.30 to 7.30 p.m. there is adoration of the Blessed Sacrament. Around this prayer and meditation, the sisters are expected to put in between ten and twelve hours of work per day in service to the poor. Once a week there is a day of recollection for the full sisters when the novices do the work for the poor (during the rest of the week, the novices have classes in

KEY FACTS

The Missionaries of Charity are a religious order founded by Mother Teresa of Calcutta. The purpose of the Missionaries of Charity is to show God's love to the poor, sick and dying. Their practice is a mixture of prayer and meditation with at least ten hours of practical work in service of the poor each day.

The practice of a religious community = what they do on a normal day.

Christian Vocation 79

Practice questions

(a) Describe the life of a particular religious community. (4)

(b) Explain why members of the community live in this way. (8)

(c) 'It's no use spending your life locked up in a monastery.' Do you agree? Give reasons for your opinion, showing that you have considered another point of view. (8)

GOOD ANSWERS TO EXAM QUESTIONS FOR CHAPTERS 7–12

Beliefs and Values

(a) What is the meaning of the word 'Christ'? (2)

The anointed or the Messiah.

(b) State what Christians believe about repentance. (6)

Christians believe that they must repent before they can be forgiven of their sins by God. By repentance they mean realising something you did was wrong, being sorry for doing it and deciding never to do it again. Catholics believe that repentance should come in the sacrament of reconciliation where a penance is done to show true repentance.

(c) Explain why the love of God is important to Christians. (8)

The love of God is important to Christians because the Bible says a lot about the love of God. It says that God loves everyone and that everyone should love God. There are some Christians who think that loving God is more important than obeying any of the commandments. In Mark's Gospel, Jesus said that the greatest commandments are to love God and love your neighbour as yourself. The *Catechism* says that the love of God is the basis of Christianity because it was God's love which sent Jesus to the world and saved people from their sins. All Christians rely on the love of God to forgive their sins and give them eternal life.

(d) 'Christian beliefs are unbelievable.' Do you agree? Give reasons for your opinion, showing that you have considered another point of view. (4)

I can see why some people would agree with this. They would say that it is difficult enough to believe in God without trying to believe that God is both three things and one thing at the same time. They may also think it is impossible to believe that Jesus was born of a virgin when it is clear that eggs cannot become foetuses without sperm.

However, I do not agree with the statement at all. It seems to me that if you believe the Bible is true then it is easy enough to believe what it says. As far as the virgin birth is concerned, if God is omnipotent, he must be able to fertilise an egg in any way he wants. As far as the Trinity is concerned, I have been taught to believe that all it means is that the one God is experienced by Christians in three different ways. So I do not agree with the statement.

Community and Tradition

(a) What does the word 'celibacy' mean? (2)

Not marrying or having sex.

(b) Outline the role of the laity in the Church. (6)

In the Catholic Church, the role of the laity is to attend church, provide for the upkeep of the church building and the priests and, most importantly, lead good Christian lives and fulfil their vocation in the world outside the Church. The laity are now expected to take part in parish and pastoral councils and take an active part in the Mass.

(c) Explain why Catholics regard Mary as the model of the Christian life. (8)

Christians believe that Mary is the model of the Christian life because Mary had an immaculate conception and lived a sinless life. Also, when the Angel Gabriel told her she had been chosen to be the mother of God she obeyed, and throughout her life she showed total obedience to God. Mary also showed Christians how to love Jesus because she loved him throughout his life and was there with him at his death. So, Mary shows Christians how to live the Christian life.

(d) 'Everybody should do what the Pope says.' Do you agree? Give reasons for your opinion, showing that you have considered another point of view. (4)

I can understand why many Catholics would agree with this statement. The Pope has been chosen by God to be the successor of St Peter, and Jesus gave St Peter the keys of the kingdom of heaven with the power to absolve people's sins. Also the Catholic Church teaches that the Pope cannot make mistakes when he speaks *ex cathedra* on matters of faith and doctrine.

However, a Catholic does not have to do what the Pope says if what he says goes against their conscience or if the Pope is not speaking *ex cathedra*. However, the main reason I disagree is that 'everybody' means other religions and other Christians as well as Catholics. I don't see why Muslims should have to do what the Pope says when Catholics don't have to do what Muslim leaders say. It would be great if all the religious leaders could get together and agree on how everyone should behave, but until then we have to accept that each religion does what its leader says, so everyone does not have to do what the Pope says.

Worship and Celebration

(a) When does Lent begin? (2)

Lent begins on Ash Wednesday.

(b) Describe the ceremony of confirmation. (6)

At a confirmation ceremony in a Catholic church, the people coming to be confirmed have to renew the vows made for them by their parents and godparents when they were baptised. Then they come forward and the bishop lays his hands on them and anoints them with chrism. There is then a special Mass.

(c) Explain the importance of the sacrament of reconciliation. (8)

The sacrament of reconciliation is also known as confession. It is extremely important for Catholics because it is the way to have forgiveness of your sins. Catholics are expected to go to Mass every week and believe you should not take the bread and wine if you have not had your sins forgiven. Also you need to be reconciled with God and have your sins forgiven if you are going to have eternal life in heaven. Clearly this is very important for Catholics as they want to go to heaven. Finally the way the sacrament works helps to clear your conscience. The priest then gives you a penance to do such as saying a number of Hail Marys or Our Fathers. If you are truly sorry for your sins and promise not to do them again, the priest gives you absolution and you know that your sins are forgiven. This gives you a clear conscience and stops you worrying.

(d) 'All babies should be baptised.' Do you agree? Give reasons for your opinion, showing that you have considered another point of view. (4)

I can see why some people would agree with this statement. Some Christians believe that people are born with original sin, and so if they die before they are baptised they will not go to heaven. It is also the teaching of many Christian Churches that babies should be baptised.

However, I disagree with the statement because I think that children should make up their own minds about being baptised. I do not see how any adult can make promises on behalf of a baby. Also the statement says 'all babies' which would mean that babies born to Buddhists, Hindus, Jews, Muslims and Sikhs should be baptised as Christians. That is absurd and so I disagree with the statement.

Living the Christian Life

(a) Name ONE of the Ten Commandments. (2)

Do not steal.

(b) Give an outline of what Jesus said about displaying religion. (6)

Jesus said that people should not make a display of their religion. He said that if they were praying, they should pray in a secret place. He said that if they were fasting, they should look happy and not let anyone know they were fasting. He said that if they were giving charity, they should do it in secret.

(c) Explain why service to others is important to Christians. (8)

Service is helping others. Jesus said that Christians should help others. In the Parable of the Sheep and the Goats, Jesus said that if people helped the starving, the homeless, the sick and those in prison, they would be helping him. In the Parable of the Good Samaritan, Jesus showed that it was not the religious people who loved their neighbour, but the Samaritan who gave his service to the man who was beaten up by robbers. This makes service very important to Christians because Christians believe Jesus was the Son of God, and Christianity is all about trying to follow Jesus and do what he did and said. If Jesus said service was important then it must be important to Christians.

Also the *Catechism* says that it is a Catholic's duty to serve others and Catholics must do what the *Catechism* says because they believe it is the Church's interpretation of God's will.

(d) 'It is easy to be a Christian today.' Do you agree? Give reasons for your opinion, showing that you have considered another point of view. (4)

I can see why some people would disagree with this statement, because they think it is difficult to carry out Jesus' commands in the modern world. For example, they would think it very hard to follow Jesus' teaching about turning the other cheek to people who attack you.

However, I agree with the statement. No one gets put in prison for being a Christian in Britain today. Indeed there are a lot of advantages to being a Christian because the Church of England is the state Church. It is easy to carry out the commands of Jesus if you really want to. There is nothing to stop you going on soup runs to help the hungry, indeed many churches organise them. It is easy to be a prison visitor and there are even Christian groups dedicated to pacifism, which have been campaigning against the war in Iraq. So I agree, it is easy to be a Christian today.

A Place of Catholic Worship

(a) Describe the main features of a particular church or cathedral. (4)

The main feature of a Catholic church is an altar with candles and a crucifix. The altar is usually in the centre of the church so everyone can see it. Next to the altar is a tabernacle which is very holy because it contains the consecrated hosts, which Catholics believe are the body of Jesus. Other features are a font for baptisms, a holy water stoop, statues of saints, a statue of the Virgin Mary with candles and a place to pray, and a statue of St Peter. Around the church are the stations of the cross to remind Catholics of the path of Jesus on Good Friday.

(b) Explain why it has these features. (8)

Catholics worship in this way because they believe that the Mass and the sacraments are the centre of life. The Mass has to follow a set form and has to be led by a priest to be effective. The sacrifice of the Mass requires an altar where the candles remind Catholics of Jesus the light of the world and the crucifix reminds them of the sacrifice of Jesus on the cross re-enacted in the Mass.

Catholics believe statues are an aid to devotion and that the saints can take prayers to God. They believe that the Virgin Mary is worthy of devotion and can pray for Christians on earth because of her immaculate conception and assumption into heaven. Because they believe in transubstantiation, Catholics believe consecrated hosts are the body of Jesus and must be kept in a tabernacle. The font is at the entrance to the church because Catholics believe baptism is the entry into membership of the Church. Catholic churches have these features because of their beliefs and many of them are not found in Protestant Churches.

(c) 'All Christians should worship together.' Do you agree? Give reasons for your opinion, showing that you have considered another point of view. (8)

Some Christians would agree with this because they think that the Church is one and therefore all denominations should worship together. They may believe in the Ecumenical Movement and belong to Churches Together, which is trying to bring the Christians of England and Wales together. They probably feel that as all Christians worship the same God and have the same beliefs about Jesus, they should all worship in the same way.

However, I disagree with them and with this statement. I would agree that the Church is one, but that does not mean that all Christians have to worship together. I cannot see why having the same beliefs means you have to worship in the same way. As a Catholic, I believe that the Mass is the best way to worship, but I can see that some Christians like to worship in different ways. If people like non-liturgical worship based on the Bible, why shouldn't they be allowed to worship in that way? It might be a good idea for all Christians to worship together once a year or so to show that they are brothers and sisters, but they should be allowed to worship in their own different ways for the rest of the year. Therefore, I disagree with the statement.

Christian Vocation

(a) Describe the life of a particular religious community. (4)

The Missionaries of Charity are a religious community founded by Mother Teresa. Their day begins with Mass followed by breakfast. Then the sisters go to work with the destitute, the dying or the lepers. They pray the rosary while they work. Then after lunch they do housework, pray the Liturgy of the Hours and then go to work again. They return at 6.30p.m. for the adoration of the Blessed Sacrament. They dine at 7.30p.m., then prepare for the next day's work and finish the day at 9.00p.m. with night prayers.

(b) Explain why members of the community live in this way. (8)

The Missionaries of Charity live this way because they were founded by Mother Teresa and she was influenced by her experiences in Calcutta. Mother Teresa became a nun in 1928 and was sent to teach Geography at the convent school in Calcutta. When she saw that many poor people were dying on the streets with no-one to care for them because they were too poor, Mother Teresa pleaded with the Calcutta City Council and was given an old Hindu temple which became known as the house of the dying. Mother Teresa brought the dying into the house and cared and prayed for them whilst they died so that they knew they were loved.

In 1950, Mother Teresa was allowed to form a new order of nuns who became the Missionaries of Charity, so they live in this way to carry on the work and beliefs of Mother Teresa. It is also their way of carrying out the command of Jesus to love God, which they do in their worship and meditation, and to love your neighbour, which they do in their practical work.

(c) 'It's no use spending your life locked up in a monastery.' Do you agree? Give reasons for your opinion, showing that you have considered another point of view. (8)

Some people would disagree with this statement because they believe that people in monasteries are leading very useful lives. St Anthony and St Benedict felt that they were taking Jesus' statement 'Take up your cross and follow me' literally by locking themselves away. Such people believe that prayer is a very powerful thing and that nuns and monks who are locked up in monasteries are doing a great deal of good by praying for the world.

However, I agree with the statement because, as far as I am concerned, to be a Christian you have to spread the Good News of Jesus by preaching and by helping the starving and all people in need. I feel that it is impossible to do this whilst locked up in a monastery and so I would say that it is no use for Christians to spend their time locked up in a monastery. Praying may help, but action is going to help more. The starving are always going to prefer to be given food than be told they are being prayed for. Jesus spent his life helping people, not locking himself in a monastery, and so I agree with the statement.